Contents

Winter peace

Spring

Summer joy

Autumn love

Tool Kit

a homemade YEAR

The Blessings of Cooking, Crafting, and Coming Together

Jerusalem Jackson Greer

PARACLETE PRESS

BREWSTER, MASSACHUSETTS

To my Sweet Man, Nathan
my wild and wonderful boys, Wylie and Miles

To my sisters, Jemimah and Judea
my brother Joshua
my parents, Tanya and Johnny
you are definitively yourselves, please stay that way.

And to Maw and Paw who always believed that I could.

This book is for you.

2013 First and Second Printing

A Homemade Year: The Blessings of Cooking, Crafting, and Coming Together

Text copyright © 2013 by Jerusalem Jackson Greer
Photographs copyright © 2013 by Judea Jackson
Scrapbooking graphics appearing throughout this book are copyright © Sahlin Studio. All rights reserved.
Craft capital letters licensed from Jacque Larsen

ISBN 978-1-61261-067-2

All Scripture quotations, unless otherwise indicated, are taken from *The Message.* Copyright © 1993, 1994, 1995, 1996, 2000, 2001, 2002. Used by permission of NavPress Publishing Group.

Scripture quotations marked NLT are taken from the Holy Bible, New Living Translation, copyright © 1996, 2004. Used by permission of Tyndale House Publisher, Inc., Wheaton, Illinois 60189. All rights reserved.
The Paraclete Press name and logo (dove and cross) are trademarks of Paraclete Press, Inc.

Library of Congress Cataloging-in-Publication Data
Greer, Jerusalem Jackson.
 A homemade year : the blessings of cooking, crafting, and coming together / Jerusalem Jackson Greer.
    pages cm
 ISBN 978-1-61261-067-2 (trade pbk.)
 1. Greer, Jerusalem Jackson. 2. Christian biography. 3. Church year meditations. 4. Handicraft. I. Title.
  BR1725.G79A3 2013
  263'.9—dc23   2012045391
ISBN 978-1-61261-067-2

10 9 8 7 6 5 4 3 2

Published by Paraclete Press
Brewster, Massachusetts
www.paracletepress.com
Printed in the United States of America

Preface

As I write this I am sitting in my parents' living room in the wee hours of the morning. The only lights come from the computer screen and the twinkling glow of the Christmas tree. I have finally settled my children down and they are fast asleep. Soon I will crawl into bed myself, snug as a bug in a rug between them. Their elbows and knees will knock and jar me all through the night. Tomorrow I will go back to our home, just sixty miles north, and they will remain here with their grandparents to ring in the New Year. Back home, their father and I will also ring in the New Year with friends and prayers and wishes almost too precious to speak out loud. My parents and the boys will join us on New Year's Day for black-eyed peas and cabbage, and soon it will be time to go back to work, back to school.

This is my favorite week. It is the week between Christmas Day and New Year's Day. It is the week when nothing has to be decided. There are no presents to buy, no big meals to cook, and no resolutions to make. And yet this is still Christmas. In fact, Christmas has only just begun.

Ten years ago I did not know what Christmastide was. I did not know about Epiphany or St. Stephen or Maundy Thursday. I had heard the terms *Candlemas* and *Michaelmas*, but I could not have picked their definitions or dates out of a liturgical calendar. In fact I did not even know what a liturgical calendar was. Growing up in a Southern Baptist family meant that the Christmas season ended on December 25 and Lent was something we picked off our black sweaters. When my family moved to Juneau, Alaska (a melting pot of beliefs and practices), my world cracked a bit wider, as I was exposed to new traditions such as Passover and Eastern Orthodoxy. Later in college and as a newlywed I found myself becoming even more curious about how others, outside of my tradition, connected to their faith daily.

In my mid-twenties, cut free from the tether of a school calendar year, I found that I was attracted to—craved, even—the rhythm, internal and external, that liturgy seemed to bring to those who leaned in and embraced it. Once I had my own children, like so many other mothers around the world, I thought long and hard about what sort of traditions I wanted our family to have. I love a great celebration. I love party decorations and special menus and taking the time to do things up right. I even love the anticipation. To me, the preparation is half the fun because it is often in the doing and preparing that the best memories are made. So I set out to find a way that would create traditions of faith for our family through the rhythm of the liturgical calendar, using fun, modern, colorful crafts and recipes. In our home I have found that even the most common tactile acts such as kneading bread dough, threading a needle, or gluing paper can be important spiritual practices, especially when paired with intentional conversations and repetition over many years. *A Homemade Year* is a book written out of this experience, and I hope it will be a yearlong guide, and sacred companion, to celebrating the rhythm of God's story through the practice and experience of the domestic arts.

Any teacher will tell you that the hardest year of teaching is the year you have to write all your lesson plans from scratch. Once the lessons are written you can use them, tweak them, and adjust them for years. But no year is ever as taxing as that first year. That is also how making this book was for me. Somehow we (my long-suffering family and friends) managed to pull off all of the crafts, parties, and recipes you see in the book in twelve months' time. I would not recommend this unless you only need three hours of sleep each night or you have a large and helpful staff, and, trust me, my family would not recommend it either. But joyfully there are several projects that we will never need to make from scratch again, because just like a classroom teacher we will be able to use them over and over for years to come, building on our experiences and memories each time.

In a recent post, blogger Penny Carothers wrote, "I've always elevated the lives of others above my own spiritual aspirations. . . . This mistaken belief parallels my long-held view that spirituality has to look a certain way to be legit." I loved reading those words, because I too have gone through seasons of thinking that legitimate spirituality only fit into one very tight-fitting box. My prayer is that *A Homemade Year* is the kind of book that will free you from just that sort of mistaken belief, from that phantom one-size-fits-all box. Instead I hope that this book inspires you to seek and experience God in a different way at your own pace. This book is meant to act as a guide, to encourage, and to teach—but never to induce guilt, to depress, or to intimidate.

As you look through this book you may find celebrations that you already observe and some that you may never have thought of. Some projects are filled with recipes, some with crafts, and some with parties. As your family grows and changes, so perhaps will how you use this book. You may try some of the recipes now, and some not for five more years. Some activities you may never even attempt until your children are grown, or you have grandchildren to entertain over the summer holidays. My traditions may not be your traditions, but perhaps they will inspire you to put a fresh spin on the ones you already practice. Perhaps also, you will find some new traditions waiting for you between these pages. There is no perfect way to use this book, but I hope you enjoy it thoroughly. And I hope that we are all able to find a way to live life being fully present in the midst of dirty dishes, laundry, and long road trips little bit by little bit. May this book be a jumping-off point from which you discover new and creative ways to experience the rhythm of God's story in your home, not just for one season, but for every season, creating joy and lasting memories in the most ordinary days.

Winter

peace

chapter 1

Advent

The Four Sundays Before December 25

> "Go," the angels said,
> "through the darkness into
> the light." And we did go.
>
> —Madeleine L'Engle,
> "The Donkey"

The thing I love most about Advent is the heartbreak. The utter and complete heartbreak. From the moment we light the first Advent candle, offering prayers of hope, until Christmas morning when I stumble out of bed, desperate for coffee, my eyes still blurry. In the living room I find my boys elbow deep in their stockings, feasting on a breakfast provided by Mr. Hershey and Old Saint Nick. For the entirety of those twenty-eight days of Advent I am filled with a bittersweet anticipation that leaves me tender, raw, and completely exposed. I haven't always loved this heartbreak that comes with Advent's arrival just as surely as Santa Claus comes to the mall and the Salvation Army comes to the street corner.

For years I tried to jolly away this ache, this deep longing that sits at the bottom of my heart, this anchor that is woven from the fibers of sorrow and broken

1

ADVENT

expectations along with the ribbons and bows of simpler times, purer joys. I was convinced that I could overcome this holiday blight, this shortcoming of belief, by giving the right gifts, making the perfect cookies, and sending the prettiest card. That I could bury, deep beneath tinsel and candy canes, the gnawing suspicion that something was unfinished. If only I could dress up my fear that all the magic of Christmas had disappeared for good with more decorations and louder twenty-four-hour carols, then maybe I could, by sheer force of will, again experience Christmas as the most wonderful time of the year.

But no matter how festive things looked on the outside, no matter how great my efforts, I could never escape the strange sadness that wound its way tightly around my heart in the early days of December. Each year, shortly after Thanksgiving, I would find myself in line somewhere (usually Target), buying something as mundane as wrapping paper and light bulbs (why am I always buying light bulbs?) when suddenly my breath would catch in my throat, and a ten-ton elephant would be sitting on my chest, making my hands shake as I struggled to pay the cashier.

Later that same day, or week, panic would suddenly rise up inside my chest, threatening to burst from my lungs in a full-force sob as I fixed another cup of homemade hot cocoa for my boys. Despite my annual cheerful attempts to muffle the heavy ache that rested just below my breastbone, the truth is, as much as I love all the hubbub (and I do love it, truly), the Advent–Christmastide season is, as the character Phillip in the 1994 movie *Mixed Nuts* so succinctly puts it, "a time when you look at your life through a magnifying glass and whatever you don't have feels overwhelming. Being alone is so much lonelier at Christmas. Being sad is so much sadder at Christmas." Truer words have never been said.

I look at my boys, Wylie and Miles, and I see that they love the Advent season unabashedly because they have the marvelous ability to suspend all disbelief. They joyfully embrace the magic, the wonder, and the hope. They *Believe* with a capital *B*. But for me, Believing is harder—the magic has dimmed and the wonder dulled. Hope and joy are almost dirty words in our cynical culture, and if I dare wish for things this year to be different, easier, happier, then I do so lightly. And so, I, and probably you too—we hold our breath and wait for it all to fall apart, half-believing that it is our very hope that will jinx the whole thing, as if our wishing will be our undoing, as if our tenderness will guarantee us heartbreak.

Last Thanksgiving, as Advent's coming rushed toward me like a freight train, I looked at my Sweet Man (my husband, Nathan) and begged to escape, to find a way to stop the train, just for a few days. To get off the hamster wheel, to take a long deep breath. I needed peace. I needed time with my boys. To smell their scruffy boy-scented necks. To hear their words, their stories. To sleep late. To move slow. To not have anything on our to-do list. To prepare my heart for Advent and all that it would bring with it. To find some space for the magic. The previous five months had been rocky and emotionally taxing for all of us. In July, I had gone from working part-time to working full-time, acquiring a new boss and co-workers in the change. As much as I loved my job, the transition was not an easy one, the change in my schedule proving to be the most challenging aspect for my little crew. I had traded in flexibility and an inconsistent paycheck for a year-round salary and rigid work hours. While I was grateful for the much-needed stability in our finances, for a job that allowed me to see my boys during the day, and for work that I enjoyed, my status as full-time working mother was like a tiny earthquake that had shifted our foundation just enough to unbalance our previous equilibrium.

By November I was mentally, physically, and emotionally worn out. My heart was exhausted, swollen and tender to the touch. The smallest prick or bump and I feared it would burst into a million pieces. I know that *Joy to the World* is a much

-loved Christmas carol, but to me the writer of *O Holy Night* put it best when he said, "the weary world rejoices." I don't know about you, but the weary world is the one I live in, and the weariest time of all seems to be Advent and Christmas. Weary from fighting the urge to keep up with the Joneses. Weary from juggling fractured families and tender emotions. Weary from working too hard and feeling as if we are still just barely scraping by each month. Weary from raising a family and doing twenty loads of laundry each week. Frankly I was weary of *being* weary.

Knowing that I would be able to spend ample time with my extended family during Christmas break, I wanted Thanksgiving week to be just our little family of four. In the words of Joni Mitchell, I was desperate for a "river to skate away on," or, at the very least, a lake view to set my heart and my spirit right for Advent's arrival. So away we went, myself, my husband, and our boys Wylie and Miles to a lakeside condo generously lent to us for the week by friends.

After our bags were unpacked and every inch of our temporary home had been inspected, discovered, and approved of, the boys and I made our way down to the lake to see what mysteries awaited us there. While they played on the muddy beach, I sat on the end of the dock, my feet dangling over the edge, grateful for the balmy—though thoroughly seasonally inappropriate—Arkansas weather that allowed my boys to roam freely outside, exploring and enjoying their freedom from school, chores, and a grumpy mother. Before long, both boys had unearthed several large sticks from the lake-bottom muck that was serving as their beach. One stick in particular caught my eye. The surface was smooth and splinter-free, having been worn down by the friction of the lake water. The stick was taller than I was, wide at the bottom and tapered at the top. But it was the branches, or rather the knobby remains of branches, that revealed the stick's true identity—a Christmas tree.

Over the past decade I have weathered many Advents in a state of unknowing. I have entered Advent seasons wondering if my marriage would be still be intact at the New Year, if the central heat would be on for Christmas, if I would have a job in January, if we would be able to afford food—let alone gifts—during November and December. I have lost friendships and a church family during an Advent season. Though all of those Advents have passed and we are better for having traveled through them, I still carry the weight, the residual scar tissue, in my heart and the knowledge that there but by the grace of God I could be again.

Each of those Advents travels with me into the next. They are like the paper-chain garlands my kids make a school. Each loop interlocked with the next loop, connected. Sitting there on the muddy bank, that old, forgotten Christmas tree looked how I felt after a decade of hard Advents. Bare. Naked. Worn down. Ravaged. Still. And to me it was the most beautiful tree I had ever seen. The most authentic. After all, was not Christ born in a barn? In the most simple, bare, ravaged way? And wasn't it through pain, through humble, imperfect circumstances, through earthly parents who themselves must have been weary, worn out, and full of uncertainty and loss, when hope came, joy arrived, and the world began again? Isn't that the true magic of Advent? Then and there I decided that somehow that tree would make it home with me. When the boys tired of the mud and our bellies cried for nourishment, I carried my tree up to the condo where it rested in a corner all week.

The rest of that trip was blissfully boring. We all slept in, I did yoga on the docks, the boys waded in the mud and water, Nathan went for long walks and baked babka, and we both drank a lot of coffee. In the evenings we anticipated the great season around the corner by watching favorite holiday movies like *Mixed Nuts*, *Elf*, and *Miracle on 34th Street*. Epic games of Monopoly and Jenga took place on the living room floor, and I even managed to get some stitching projects finished. Each day I found that I could breathe a little deeper, think a little clearer, see a little further.

Thanksgiving Day came and we cooked a great feast full of nontraditional foods. Nathan made his version of Chef Tessa Kiros's pork fillet in pastry with wild mushrooms and cream sauce, which was so perfectly rich and smooth that I can still taste it, the subtle mushroom flavors mixing with the buttery crust, perhaps the most delicious dish I have ever eaten. I made a puff pastry appetizer (we believe in the healing powers of carbs, as you can tell) from the Thanksgiving issue of *Martha Stewart Living* that was filled with ingredients such as artichokes, Dijon mustard, and red wine. Right out of the oven, each bite exploded in my mouth—tangy, creamy, acidic. Even writing about them makes me crave them more. Wylie made, almost entirely on his own, a ricotta tart with a chocolate crust. The condo was not stocked for gourmet cooking, but instead held only the bare basics of kitchen utensils and supplies. For folks accustomed to KitchenAid mixers, specialty gadgets, and a plethora of good pots and pans, attempting these recipes with our ragtag supplies was a fun challenge. We rolled our dough out with wine bottles, took turns whipping things into submission relay-style, and made a trip to Wal-Mart for some disposable pans to bake our Thanksgiving dressing (our one concession to the traditional meal) in.

Soon the week was over, and it was time to head home. I crammed my naked Christmas tree on top of bags of dirty clothes and board games, shut the hatch, climbed in the passenger seat, and we drove away. Back to school, back to work, Advent and Christmas waiting for us on the other side of our front door.

Shauna Niequist, in her 2010 book *Bittersweet: Thoughts on Change, Grace, and Learning the Hard Way,* writes: "When life is sweet, say thank you and celebrate. And when life is bitter, say thank you and grow." This is the essence of Advent to me. When it is sweet, I am to say "thank you" and celebrate, and when it is less than sweet, I will still say "thank you" and I will do my best to grow. Because honestly, between the parties and the presents and the decorating and holly jolliness of it all, I have no energy left for pretending that everything always has been and always will be fine. Advent is hard, and it often leaves me undone. Pretending that I need anything other than holy healing and redemption is a lie. To dress my mantel with anything other than a garland of humility and a wreath of thankfulness is to invite the worst kind of self-pity and disappointment.

Of course Advent is bittersweet! Of course it is weary and raw and emotional. It began that way, with the words of an angel to an unwed teenage girl, words that changed her life and ours. And so like Mary, traveling a dirty, dusty road to Bethlehem, Advent is when I wait in utter anticipation that one will come who will save me and change the world. One who will right wrongs, bind up wounds, wipe away tears. I will wait for him because I have reached the end of my rope and I cannot save anyone, let alone myself. It is now, at Advent, that I am given the chance to suspend all expectation for the entire season and instead to revel in the mystery; to give myself permission to hold both sadness and joy, sorrow and hope, disappointment and peace in the same heart and to wait for the night when the world will, and does, begin again, revealing the wondrous, glorious morn.

Woodland Advent Wreath

When I lived in Juneau, Alaska, I was introduced for the first time to the Advent wreath. Typically the Advent wreath, a tradition that helps Christians observe the four Sundays of Advent as they journey toward Christmas, is made from evergreens. But as with most things in Southeast Alaska, the Advent wreath that our new church family introduced to us was not typical of the sort of wreath you might find in the "lower forty-eight." Our wreath, made from a thick slice of log, was as unique, beautiful, and unexpected as Alaska itself. Drawing inspiration from those log bases, I have made our family our own woodland Advent wreath.

Now, this may cause some people to raise their liturgical-tradition eyebrows, but I do not use the traditional purple and pink candles for our wreath. Instead, we use candles in colors that I love. (I blame my contrary, evangelical genetics for this.) Not to be too casual about this very important tradition, each separate color of candle still represents one aspect of our Advent observance, helping provide guidance as we move through the month. Of course if you are a fan of the original colors (three purple, one rose, one white) you can easily substitute those instead. Below I have noted both my color choice and the traditional color choices for each week.

Materials Needed

- Slice of a log, 1½–2 inches thick, about 10 inches in diameter

- 5 tall candles (dinner or taper)
  My color choices: 1 lime green, 1 light pink, 1 red, 1 light blue, and 1 white
  Traditional color choices: 3 purple, 1 light pink or rose, and 1 white

- Electric hand drill with 1-inch bit

- 80-grit sandpaper

Directions

Carefully slice your log to the correct thickness, using a chain saw and safety goggles. If you cannot find or cut your own log, you should be able to visit a local Christmas tree farm or find someone who sells firewood who can cut your log for you.

Once the log is sliced, sand both sides and the edges with your sandpaper. (When the log is sliced the bark will naturally begin to fall off. You can leave it rough and patchy or you can sand it down for a smoother edge.)

Drill 1 1-inch hole directly in the middle, going almost the entire way through the log slice.

Drill four more holes the same way, in the positions of north, south, east, and west (see wreath picture for example).

Once this is done, add your four colorful candles to the four outlying holes and one white candle in the middle. Each week when your family gathers to light the candle, have children bring the item to represent each week's theme (see below) to place on the wreath, next to the corresponding candle.

ADVENT

Lighting the Advent Candles at Home

Here are the readings, the quotes, and the order that our family follows for Advent. We read these words as we light the candles each Sunday night at our dinner table. Only the first candle is lit on the first Sunday, then the first and second on the next Sunday, until all the candles are lit on Christmas Eve. We try to divide responsibilities up according to the interest and ability of each family member, giving everyone at least one task. For instance, younger children can place the ornaments, and older children can light the candles or read the Scriptures. The order of themes and historical connections that we follow may not be the same as those of your faith family, as there is a variety of traditions across the Christian community. We have chosen the order that fits our family observance best, and I would encourage you to do the same.

First Sunday in Advent

Theme: *Hope*

Historical connection: Patriarchs (Abraham and the Old Testament ancestors of Christ)

Color: Green or purple

Item: Greenery/Moss

Old Testament Reading: Isaiah 11:1–10

New Testament Reading: Romans 5:1–5

Quote: "Hope begins in the dark, the stubborn hope that if you just show up and try to do the right thing, the dawn will come." (Anne Lamott, *Bird by Bird: Some Instructions on Writing and Life*)

Offer a prayer of hope on behalf of those who have run out of hope. Pray that their hearts will be opened and that they can Believe again.

Second Sunday in Advent

Theme: *Love*

Historical connection: Prophets (those in both the Old and New Testaments who foretold the birth of Christ)

Color: Red or purple

Item: Heart (perhaps a rock in this shape)

Old Testament Reading: Jeremiah 33:10

New Testament Reading: 1 Corinthians 13:1–8

Quote: "God does not make clones; each person is different, a tribute to God's creativity. If we are to love our neighbor as ourself, we must accept people as they are." (Father Henry Fehren, *Good News for Alienated Catholics*)

Offer a prayer for those who may not believe they are worth being loved; pray that they will feel the love of Christ in a miraculous way this Christmas.

Third Sunday in Advent

Theme: *Joy*

Historical connection: John the Baptist

Color: Blue or pink

Item: Bell

Old Testament Reading: Isaiah 52:7–15

New Testament Reading: Luke 1:1–25

Quote: "Joy is prayer—Joy is strength—Joy is a net of love by which you can catch souls." (Mother Teresa, *A Gift for God: Prayers and Meditations*)

Offer a joyful prayer of thanksgiving for all those who give their life to serving others as Christ's hands and feet on earth.

Fourth Sunday in Advent

Theme: *Peace*

Historical connection: Mary (mother of Jesus)

Color: Pink or purple

Item: Dove (perhaps one that is cut out of paper or an ornament)

Old Testament Reading: Isaiah 7:10–17

New Testament Reading: Luke 1:26–56

Quote: "Peace is a daily, a weekly, a monthly process, gradually changing opinions, slowly eroding old barriers, quietly building new structures." (John F. Kennedy, in a speech to the United Nations, September 25, 1961)

Offer a prayer for all those who live in war-torn neighborhoods or abusive homes. Pray that God's healing will bind up their wounds and that they will know peace in their time.

Christmas Eve

Theme: *Savior*

Historical connection: Birth, ministry, death, and resurrection of Christ

Color: White

Item: Star

Old Testament Reading: Isaiah 9:6–7

New Testament Reading: Luke 2:1–20

Quote: "The world is not as just, not as loving, not as whole as we know it can and should be. But the coming of Christ and his presence among us—as one of us—give us reason to live in hope: that light will shatter the darkness, that we can be liberated from our fears and prejudices, that we are never alone or abandoned."
(*Connections* Magazine, 11/28/93)

Together, offer this "Christmas Eve Prayer" by Robert Louis Stevenson:

> Loving God, Help us remember the birth of
>   Jesus, that we may share in the song of the
>   angels,
> the gladness of the shepherds,
> and worship of the wise men.
> Close the door of hate
> and open the door of love all over the world.
> Let kindness come with every gift and good
>   desires with every greeting.
> Deliver us from evil by the blessing which
>   Christ brings,
> and teach us to be merry with clear hearts.
>
> May the Christmas morning make us happy to
>   be thy children,
> and Christmas evening bring us to our beds
>   with grateful thoughts,
> forgiving and forgiven, for Jesus' sake.
> Amen.

Countdown-to-Christmas Garland Advent Calendar

This Advent calendar, made from shipping tags, is something we have been using in our home for several years now. I created the calendar with the instructions and encouragements on the back because I wanted a way to count down the days from December 1 to Christmas Day that would be both interactive and somewhat challenging for all of us.

There are a lot of great Advent calendars on the market, but at the time that I made this my budget for decorations was less than zero. So I looked around our house and foraged in my craft stash for supplies until I found tags, glue, and leftover ribbons. If you decide to make this craft, either by yourself or with your kids, I encourage you to use what you have on hand and to enjoy the process, and above all—do not worry about perfection. Just have fun creating a calendar that will inspire and challenge as you and your family travel from Advent to Christmas. Some of our family's most challenging tags are the ones that remind us to be kind to those who annoy or frustrate us. The tags we find the most delight in are the ones that remind us to slow down and enjoy being together, whether that means watching a classic holiday movie or sitting around the kitchen table drinking hot chocolate together.

Materials Needed

- 25 large shipping tags (purchased at an office supply store)
- Glue sticks
- Printer or copier
- Scissors (regular and pinking shears)
- Scrapbook papers in a variety of Christmas colors and patterns of your choosing
- Ribbon or pompom trim cut into 3 1-yard lengths
- Hole punch
- 25 small ornaments
- 25 small lengths of string or 25 ornament hooks

Directions

To begin, copy or print the numbers and daily challenges from the patterns in chapter 23.

Next, cut these out in 1¾-inch squares, making sure to keep the corresponding days with the corresponding challenges.

Cut out 50 2-inch squares from your selection of scrapbook paper, using your pinking shears.

Glue the scrapbook paper squares to the center of the shipping tags, front and back. Next, glue the numbers and the daily challenges into the center of the scrapbook paper squares on each side, creating a layering effect.

Punch a hole in the bottom of each tag about ½-inch up from the edge.

Cut your ribbon or pompom fringe into three even strands of 12 inches each. Hang your strands on the wall, and then tie each of the tags to the three strands.

Tie 8 of the tags to the top strand, 9 tags to the middle

strand, and 8 tags to the lower strand. (If you prefer, you can hang them all on one really long strand instead of dividing them into threes.)

After your tags have been tied to the strands of ribbon, attach (either with string or an ornament hook) a small ornament to each shipping tag. Make sure all the tags are turned so that the numbers are facing out and can be seen.

Starting on December 1, help your kids turn one number per day, reading together the daily challenge on the back. Leave each challenge facing outward as you move toward December 25. Each day, after you have turned the number, help your kids remove the small ornament that is attached to the shipping tag. Have your children hang the ornament on either a small tree, perhaps near the Advent garland, or on the larger family tree. This small act of adding an ornament a day to a tree is just one way that your kids can engage and interact with this garland. Even toddlers can help with ornaments and feel a part of the daily celebration of Advent and the anticipation as you move together toward Christmas Day.

ADVENT

chapter 2

St. Lucy's Day

> There are two ways of spreading light:
> To be the candle or the mirror that reflects it.
> —Edith Wharton, *Vesalius in Zante*

A few weeks ago the light changed. More specifically we fell back an hour at the end of daylight saving time, and so now we are all living as if the light changed, when really we are the ones who changed. All of us, together, by a general consent have changed our rhythms and habits. But still the light changed, regardless of why, and the air quickly followed suit. Advent is now underway, and the kids have begun their anxious countdown to Christmas morning. In the late afternoon, as I leave work, there is a hazy glow that covers the city, light coming from the long and winding stream of cars crossing the bridge, traveling away from downtown, heading back home, their taillights reflecting off the late autumn clouds. Winter has started its slow descent.

In the later afternoon, home after a long day, I will walk around the house turning on all the lights and the Christmas tree, breaking up the darkness that has crept inside while we were all away at work and school. Going out to check the mail, I turn and notice how bright our house looks from the street, how I can see bits of life happening through the gaps where the curtains are not pulled closed. I can see Wylie at the dining room table finishing homework, Nathan in the kitchen rinsing out a glass, and I know that somewhere Miles is inside, conducting an experiment or creating some other version of creative mischief. Our little home glows and hums in the premature darkness with a day not finished, and I am reminded of a night, similar to this one, and another house lit up with holiday cheer from the inside out.

Over the course of my childhood my family moved several times as my father finished college, then seminary, and tried to find his footing as a Southern Baptist pastor. My mother, the Laverne to his Shirley, was a free spirit and stay-at-home momma. Because of their chosen professions our bank account was often low, and this, together with my off-and-on-again homeschooled status and my father's job title, created a thin, frosted glass wall of separation between me and other children. Making friends was always a little precarious, because inevitably, as is normal for preteen girls, my friends would want to have a sleepover. Being a typical overly self-conscious adolescent I was painfully aware of each little eccentricity that my family possessed, and I was fearful of the ridicule I might be subjected to if my mother enforced one of her not-cool rules on us. For instance, she had rules about what we could and could not watch on TV. No *Smurfs* (there was a wizard). No *Scooby-Doo* (too many ghosts). No *Dukes of Hazzard* (have you seen Daisy's shorts?). Sitcoms such as *Gimme a Break!* (too much negativity) and even *Who's the Boss?* were questionable with that "unmarried man and women" potential for trouble always lurking.

The friends I did bring home were few, and only after I had assessed if they liked me enough to weather an unpredictable evening at my house, with my hippie Christian mother, pastor father, and three younger and very active siblings who would attach themselves to my friends' hips as soon as they entered the door. My mother insisted that we all eat dinner together, around the table. There was no eating take-out pizza safely hidden in my bedroom, with the radio turned up loud. If a friend came over to my house, she would have to endure a family meal.

While I was growing up our family ate breakfast and supper (and often lunch) together around our kitchen table, Monday through Friday and Sundays. Each night my mother insisted that we gather around the table and eat a hot meal together, and so we traveled with her through a variety of culinary explorations, inspired by both her reading choices and her budget. There were the successes: tender, fried pork chops with smashed potatoes and gravy, her perfect Christmas ham, and my favorite dish of sausage and peppers over a bed of sticky rice. And then there were the failures: the beet soufflé for Valentine's Day, the cold cucumber soup that my dad warmed up in the microwave, and the rubbery squid pizza. Of course only now that I am a mother myself do I appreciate the sheer tenacity it must have taken her to cook meal after meal after meal, for a less than grateful audience. But it was when I left to go to college that I discovered the wisdom of my mother's dedication to the shared evening meal.

Standing in the Wal-Mart line with my mother in Arkadelphia, Arkansas, our cart filled with all the last-minute essentials that are ubiquitous to college freshmen, it suddenly hit me—my mother was going home and I was staying behind. I would be alone. By myself. Sure, I had a roommate, but who was she? What if I didn't like her? Worse, what if she didn't like me? Who would I eat dinner with? When would I go to dinner? How would I choose a table? Visions of me completely frozen in the cafeteria sprung to mind, followed by visions of me and my tray being knocked over by linebacker seniors, resulting in mass hysterical laughter from all the other students. For one brief moment I considered calling it quits and hitching a ride back to Alaska in my mother's suitcase.

Luckily fate intervened, and within hours of hugging my mother goodbye and walking back into my dorm room, tears choked back in my throat, I acquired seven girlfriends who are still my friends, some of them my very closest friends, to this day. My freshman year of college was ridiculously wonderful, which makes people who didn't love college irritated whenever I bring it up. But it is true. I loved all of college, and I mourned the loss of that life for at least a year after graduation. But even as good as all five years were, that first year and especially that first semester holds a special place in my heart because of the friendships I found in Jeanetta, Joanne, Julie, Sarah, Shari, Mandi-with-an-*i*, and Mandy-with-a-*y*.

Because we attended a Southern Baptist university, it was not surprising that most of the girls were daughters of missionaries and church staff members themselves, creating an instantaneous camaraderie among us. There were so many things that I did not have to explain to them, things they just understood intuitively. Many of their mothers also had funny rules about things like watching *Scooby-Doo* (no) and going to school dances (no again) and swimsuits (one-piece only). Together we experienced bits of culture shock, homesickness, and the emerging formation of our adult selves. We gained the freshmen fifteen, had open-closet policies, and each night at 5:00 PM sharp we met in Mandy-with-a-*y* and Joanne's room to walk together, like a gaggle of geese, across the parking lot between our dorm and the cafeteria, to eat dinner all together (where I am proud to say I never dropped my tray).

Over the next few months, our friendships solidified. In December we decided that we would all travel an hour north to my grandparents' home for a Christmas weekend celebration together before finals, before we all headed home for Christmas break. My grandparents' house, set on a lovely wooded lot overlooking a small lake inlet, had plenty of room for my friends and me, and my sweet Maw and Paw, sensing they would be outnumbered, generously offered to let us have the whole place to ourselves. We happily conceded on one condition—that they let us, as a gift for their hospitality, decorate their home for the holidays. They agreed and the deal was made. We packed our bags with way too many hair dryers, curling irons, and bottles of Final Net for one weekend where we would see no boys, crammed ourselves into the few cars we had among us, and headed to the woods for a wild weekend of cookie-eating and garland-swagging.

Once safely locked in the house, every light turned on (causing the neighbors to worry for my grandparents' electric bill), we took turns calling our boyfriends using our calling cards. Bags barely unloaded, and the tape deck located, the girls got to work decorating. Shari and Mandy-with-a-*y* took the front porch, wrapping anything that stood still in white lights, tinsel garland, and red bows. Jeanetta, Julie, and Sarah decorated the small tree Paw had cut down the night before. Mandi-with-an-*i* strung green garland all along the tops of the dining room windows, and Joanne helped me prepare our Christmas feast in the kitchen. Poor as a college mouse, I wanted to give them each a wonderful Christmas gift, but all I could think of was to follow my mother's lead: fix a meal, cook the best dishes I knew, and gather everyone around the table. So I covered the table in my favorite comfort foods—pesto with toasted pine nuts and feta cheese over angel hair pasta and my version of stromboli, stuffed with chopped pepperoni, ham, olives, green peppers, and provolone cheese and baked inside Italian bread dough. Looking around the table, as we gave thanks to our Maker for this food and each other, I realized that in one beautiful semester these girls had gone from just being my friends to being my family, my sisters.

Eighteen Christmases have passed since that first December, and while we still gather together, in whatever form we can muster each year, that first gathering will always remain the most magical. The tree shining through the gauzy curtains. The branches covered in vintage ornaments made from bits of felt covered in sequins, old glass balls almost transparent from years of use, and strands of tinsel icing spread thickly over the entire tree, all reflecting the glow from the tiny light bulbs. I can see Sarah, wrapped in my great-grandmother's quilt, dancing around the kitchen. I see Shari wrapped in tinsel garland on the porch, trying to untangle the strands of lights. I see Jeanetta's fiery eyes flashing when Mandy played a practical joke on her. I see Julie and Joanne setting the dining room table, Mandi making herself a PB&J sandwich, a little leery of the pesto. I see all of us eighteen years young, no clue about the ways our paths would diverge and converge over the next two decades, oblivious to the heartbreaks we would endure, the miracles we would witness, the choices we would be faced with, and the ways Christ would work his redeeming grace through all of our stories over the next eighteen years of Advents.

As predictable as decorating the tree, a moment arrives each Advent when I realize that I have once again lost sight of what makes the season holy and set apart. My focus has slipped from Christ and shifted to my bank account, all the gifts I still have to buy or make, and all the parties I still have to host or attend. My first reaction is to give over to feelings of guilt—to give up all hope of having a meaningful Christmas season and just join in the consumer rat race. But in the middle of all the hustle and bustle, just as I am tempted to pitch over the edge in holiday desperation and frantic people-pleasing, along comes St. Lucy, calm, serene, and full of purpose. With her traditional Scandinavian wreath of candles crowning her head, she brings light to the darkness of early winter. I read her words in *Ælfric's Life of St. Lucy*: "You can take nothing with you from this life, and whatever you give away at death for the Lord's sake you give because you cannot take it with you. Give now to the true Savior, while you are healthy, whatever you intended to give away at your death," and I am gently reminded that it is not just material gifts that I need to give away, but also those things that are most precious to me: my time, my laughter, my friendship, my love, my attention, my prayers. These are the gifts that will last, will take root and grow over the years, will mean more in twenty years' time than they even mean today. These are the gifts that sustain us through the heartbreaks and the changes that we cannot have foreseen, that allow us to rejoice without envy or pettiness at the blessings that others receive. These are the same gifts that my mother gave our family daily and that the girls and I gave to each other, across the dinner table, all those Christmases ago.

Holly Jolly Serving Tray and St. Lucy's Sweet Orange Rolls

My mother's family knows the value of taking life slowly, with languid mornings and midday naps. Not that they are lazy or unproductive—quite the opposite, in fact. They just have a better sense than most people about when to get their panties in a bunch, and when to sit on the porch swing sipping their coffee instead. It should come as no surprise then that breakfast in bed was a regular occurrence at both my parents' and grandparents' home. I can remember Sunday mornings at my grandparents', when Paw would bring Maw and me steamy bowls of oatmeal swimming in butter, a thick sugary crust gathering along the edges. Tiny cups of milk and juice along with half a grapefruit, scored and ready to eat, completed the meal, which was lovingly presented on a metal tray Paw would place on top of the pillow laid ready in my lap.

Scandinavian countries such as Sweden and Denmark celebrate St. Lucy's Day with several lovely traditions, but I think my favorite is the breakfast in bed that children bring to their parents. A tray covered with coffee and sweet breakfast buns sounds like the perfect way to start a cold winter morning during the busiest time of the year.

23

Serving Tray

Materials Needed

- Decoupage glue
- Magazines and catalogs (ones that you are willing to cut up)
- Sponge paintbrush (or other small brush)
- Scissors
- Sturdy, inexpensive (or vintage) sheet pan (any shape)

Directions

Gather any magazines, catalogs, and other ephemera that you don't mind cutting up and gluing down. Look for images that remind you of Christmas and winter.

Once you have chosen and cut your images, start laying them out on your cookie sheet or pizza pan, making sure to gather different shapes and sizes. Make your decoupage collage as random or symmetrical as pleases you.

Remember you can overlap pictures as needed, and add smaller ones on top of larger ones. Layering is encouraged!

Using your decoupage glue, give the back of your images a light coating and place in pan.

After gluing your pictures down, smooth out the bubbles using your fingers or a brayer tool.

Next generously but gently coat the top of your images and pan, continuing to gently smooth out any wrinkles with your fingers or brayer tool. Your fingers may get sticky (a common by product of good crafting), so it is helpful to keep a small dish of water and a damp washcloth nearby while you work.

Let your tray dry at least twenty-four hours. If you think you will give your tray a good workout serving food and drinks over the course of the holiday season, coat the tray with decoupage glue at least two more times for added protection. Make sure to let each layer dry thoroughly before applying the next one. (You don't want a goopy, sticky tray on your hands.)

25

ST. LUCY'S DAY

St. Lucy's Sweet Orange Rolls

In some Scandinavian countries it is customary to make a breakfast bun that is flavored with saffron for the St. Lucy's Day breakfast. At our house we like sweet rolls, primarily because we don't keep a lot of saffron on hand. Another reason is that very often December 13 rolls around during the school and work week, and by using several prepared items that can be found easily at our local grocery store, I save time and energy that can be better spent enjoying my family.

Ingredients

1½ tablespoons butter

1   large tube of prepared flaky
     cinnamon roll dough
     Icing package that comes
     with your rolls

1   cup chopped walnuts

1   teaspoon orange juice or
     the juice from 1 mandarin
     orange

1   teaspoon orange zest
     (about half of 1 orange or 1
     whole mandarin orange)

Directions

- Preheat the oven to 400 degrees.
- Thoroughly grease inside edges and bottom of pie pan with butter or cooking spray.
- Cut 1 tablespoon of butter into small pats and place randomly in bottom of pan. In a small bowl mix together the premade icing, juice, ½ tablespoon melted butter, and orange zest to make a glaze. Warm in microwave for 40 seconds.
- Pour your glaze in the bottom of the pan, spreading it around as you pour.
- Next add the chopped nuts covering the glaze.

Place cinnamon rolls on top of nut/glaze mixture, cinnamon side down. They will be touching. Bake until the rolls are golden (about 15–20 minutes). Remove from oven and let cool. After buns have cooled, flip them out on a plate and serve.

27

chapter 3

Christmas Day

> He did whistle and she did sing
> On Christmas day, on Christmas day
> He did whistle and she did sing
> On Christmas day in the morning
> —"I Saw Three Ships" (a traditional English Christmas carol)

The first time I gave birth I was twenty-five (almost twenty-six) years old. My labor was long, my birth plan a mess, and the crowd outside my door circus-like. But eventually, after about twenty-four hours, Wylie came into this world, and I adored him from the moment I held him. From the moment his fingers, looking so much like his father's, grabbed mine - I was hooked. His eyes were so serious and intense as he looked up at me, as if he were trying to match my odd, blurry image together with my familiar voice. But, despite this love and adoration, despite that I knew him and he knew me from the moment I held him cheek to cheek, I did not yet know what it meant to be a mother. What it meant to raise a son. These things were still beyond my experience, beyond what I could read in books or learn from older mothers. They were the sorts of things I would have to learn for myself.

The second time I gave birth it was different. Three years later, seven months into my second pregnancy, I realized with great shock that I would have to go

through labor again. That the pain was inevitable. That despite the medicines and the breathing techniques and all the preparations I could muster, I was still going to birth a human into this world, his body from mine, blood and pain and tearing all being part of the deal. For about thirty seconds I wanted to take it all back. I wanted to stop time and stay seven months' pregnant forever.

When the day came for Miles's arrival, there were only five of us in the delivery room: one nurse, my mother, my doctor, and my husband. There were no friends waiting outside the door, no time for a crowd to gather as they had during Wylie's birth. This time my labor progressed much more quickly, partially because I now knew how my body worked and what it needed, how to help Mother Nature out with her task. For fifteen minutes I pushed as hard as I could. Willing my body to do its job even when the epidural blocked so much feeling. "Work. Push!" I silently screamed to myself, closing my eyes, gripping Nathan's hands, praying the message was traveling the path throughout my synapses to where it needed to be. Suddenly, there was a release of pressure and I heard a scrawny cry for air. Miles had made it.

I looked up at my son and burst into salty tears that ran down my cheeks as I lay back and waited to hold him. My tears were tears of relief and joy. And of responsibility. This time, unlike the first time I gave birth, I knew what it meant to have a son. To be a mother. The pain and the cost. The fear. The love. This time I knew what it meant to bring another human into this world. I knew what it meant to have "a piece of my heart walking around outside my body," to paraphrase author Elizabeth Stone. I knew that I would fight to keep him safe, to love him and raise him as only I knew how; that I would not be perfect, that I would fail him in a million little ways, but that I would do my best, crazy as it would seem at times.

Six hours would pass before I was able to hold my baby close, examine all his fingers and toes for myself. Six excruciatingly long hours until I could hear his cry, tend to him as a mother should, change him and feed him, feel his skin against my skin. Miles was born with fluid in his lungs and had to be taken to the neonatal intensive care unit. For the first time in nine months we were physically separated from each other, and the gulf was wide.

When I was less than a year old, my father left the U.S. Air Force in order to finish his college education and then to attend seminary. As far back as I can remember, my father has been a Southern Baptist pastor in some capacity, and during my middle childhood years, it was his only vocation; but at heart he is an introverted poet, scholar, and musician, and he never sought the role of senior pastor of a mega-church, never climbed the church leadership ladder. This also meant that our bank account did not climb any ladders, either. For herself, my mother chose to be a stay-at-home mother as her vocation, homeschooling all four of us for a large chunk of our education and creating an amazing environment for creativity. But even though this was what she wanted, what she chose—it was still *work*, and even though she wasn't bringing in a paycheck, she still had financial responsibilities. So, the task to find ways to stretch one paycheck as far and as wide as the Atlantic Ocean fell to her.

Despite our cheese-and-crackers budget, we always had gifts under the tree—maybe not many, but there was *always* something lovely: something my mother had stayed up and sewn through the night; something she had saved pennies or Green Stamps to purchase. Once, during the Cabbage Patch Kid phase, she even took a night sewing class in order to make me an extra-large soft-headed Cabbage Patch knockoff doll, just what I had wished for. (Curiously, I had wanted only a boy doll and that Christmas I got two—one my mother made and one off-brand doll that my grandmother bought me. Talk about foreshadowing!) Even my father, who loves to shop for gifts almost as much as his father, got in on the thrifty gift-giving, and my most favorite gifts from him were always things that were given with more thought than cash.

The big family gift that first Christmas in Juneau was a videocassette recorder. Months before Christmas, my parents had purchased and hidden it in my father's office at the church. During those weeks leading up to Christmas, Daddy secretly videotaped television shows and movies for each of us, wrapping up the videotapes and putting them under the tree, so that come Christmas morning my three siblings and I would each have something special to watch. My tape was filled with the PBS *Anne of Green Gables* series, based on the books by Lucy Maud Montgomery, and within five minutes of viewing I knew had found a bosom buddy for life in Anne. I am sure there were many things on my Christmas wish list that year that I was convinced I needed, that I spent nights dreaming of and hoping for. But I have no idea what they were, and chances are I will never remember, but I will remember Anne of Green Gables forever—she became a huge part of my identity. As dramatic as it sounds to say, I would not be who I am today if it had not been for Anne, and I have my daddy and his thrifty thoughtfulness to thank for that.

I wonder now, a parent myself, trying to scrimp and save in preparation for Christmas gifts and decorations, staying up late to put the final stitches in a gift, juggling the electric bill with the boys' wish lists, if my parents ever second-guessed their choices. If they ever felt that homespun gifts and home-taped videos were second-rate gifts. If they ever wondered if they had made the right choices, traveled the right path. I wonder those things about myself all the time—isn't that part of parenting? The never knowing if you are getting it right? You hope you are, you want to desperately, but you never know for sure. "Please Lord, just let the good stuff stick," I pray.

I take some solace in the fact that despite how I acted then, what matters now, what has stayed with me all these years about our family's Christmas, was not when or how our tree was set up, or what presents I didn't get, or how odd the gifts I did get might have turned out to be. What I am grateful for now, even as I put my own children's inadequate gifts under the tree, is that regardless of whatever was not enough, what was always in full supply on Christmas Day was my parents' love and presence. Come Christmas morning our home was full of merriment, laughter, and kisses; there was always hot food on the table, a dry roof over our heads, plenty of books to read, and music to dance to. We had each other, despite whatever other brokenness our lives encountered.

A few years ago my husband, Nathan, and his band recorded a version of the traditional Christmas tune *"I Saw Three Ships."* The version of lyrics they chose includes a verse about Joseph and his lady, celebrating sweetly on Christmas Day. That year was a particularly lean one for our little family, and as I decorated our small tree, listening to their recording over and over, I thought about Mary and Joseph, doing their best to care for their child as well. How scary and uncertain everything must have felt those first few years. How could they know if they were doing the right things, making the best choices? Starting off marriage with baby God, the appearances of angels, death decrees, and starting over in a foreign land—none of those things were normal or expected. How could they have predicted this life?

For Mary and Joseph, in the thirty-three years between the birth of Jesus and his death, Christmas wasn't Christmas; instead, it was simply their boy's birthday. A day to remember all the strange and wonderful circumstances of his birth, a day to celebrate that they had survived the turmoil that surrounded his arrival. They had kept their boy safe from Herod's death orders, somehow making it safely to Egypt— perhaps even escaping in a fleet of three ships. For Mary, Joseph, and little boy Jesus, the day would have been one to dance a lively dance, and sing a happy song, to retell the stories of their wondrous adventure. A time to rejoice that, despite whatever else may be broken or strange, despite all the ways they may be different from other families, however odd their story, they were still a family—they had survived. And as I sing along to "He did whistle and she did dance," I think so should we, on "Christmas Day in the morning" and all year long.

CHRISTMAS DAY

Felt Ornament Gift Embellishments

When I was a little girl my mother taught me that it is not the size of the bow that makes the statement, but the size of the bow's tail. "Everyone thinks that the beauty of a bow is all in the loop size," she said one December evening as she was helping me tie some ribbon on a wreath, "but really what makes a bow pretty is how long and lovely the tails are." She also taught me to be resourceful and thrifty. So although I want my gifts to be lovely, I do not want to blow my whole budget on paper and bags and cards that will most likely get tossed in the trash. Instead I try to find useful wrapping—a cookie cutter instead of a bow, a jar that can be repurposed. This year I wanted to replace the bows with ornaments that each person could keep, a little extra gift, the cherry on the top. I also wanted to keep the cost down and the basic wrapping simple and I wanted to let the ornaments speak for themselves.

Materials Needed

- 8 x 11-inch sheets of felt
- Craft glue
- Scissors
- Glitter
- Thin paintbrush
- Hole punch
- Cookie cutters in Christmas as well as circles and animal shapes
- Ink pen
- Hot glue
- Pipe cleaners
- Jingle bells

Directions

Using your ink pen, trace the cookie cutter shapes onto the felt. Position your tracings so that you can get the most out of each sheet of fabric.

Cut your shapes out and punch a hole in the top of each.

With a paintbrush, apply glue to the edges, sprinkle with glitter, and let dry.

Glue any pieces that you need to join together with your hot glue gun (for instance, holly leaves and berries).

Layer shipping tags or other vintage paper ephemera underneath the ornaments for added texture.

Attach the ornaments to your gift boxes using twine, ribbon, or pipe cleaners, and finish the whole embellishment off with a jingle bell or two secured to your ribbon or twine.

chapter 4

St. Stephen's Day

"The real things haven't changed. It is still best to be honest and truthful; to make the most of what we have; to be happy with simple pleasures; and have courage when things go wrong."
—Laura Ingalls Wilder,
"Open Letter to Children"

Our first night camping at Petit Jean State Park, we didn't get to camp till late. As much as we love camping, we haven't learned how to do it quickly, simply, or cheaply. Just getting to our campsites always seems to take an Act of Congress. There is the packing, in which we pack our car so full it looks like we are moving cross-country instead of just driving north for a couple of hours and staying two nights. We take regular blankets instead of sleeping bags (we are a wiggly crew) and vintage but unbreakable dishes instead of paper (prettier and better for the environment). Then there are the books: we can't seem to leave without each packing a backpack of books. We feel naked without a copious amount of reading materials around us at all times, even if we never crack a book on the entire trip. Finally there are the

35

things that we forgot to pack, or didn't have to time to shop for, or didn't anticipate needing (for example, when it snowed during our spring break camping trip and we suddenly needed to find a space heater quickly).

Once we had set up camp and finished unloading our car, we headed back down the mountain to hit up Wal-Mart for all the things we had forgotten or were out of and to find a local restaurant to have dinner, as we were too far behind schedule to cook at camp. By the time we returned to our campsite the sky was pitch black and everyone was worn out and cranky, the end of a long day finally overpowering our excitement. Our camping trips always smack a little of a *National Lampoon* movie, and in true Griswold fashion we had made the mistake of not mapping out our way to the bathrooms before it got dark, so that by the time we really needed to find them we couldn't. Nathan, in a resourceful gesture, finally scrounged up a map of the park, locating the bathhouses on the other side of the woods that sat behind our tent. Leaving the boys with me, he headed off with only a small flashlight, making his way through an overgrown path in the woods that he believed would cut through to the bathrooms. Twenty minutes later he returned with all his limbs intact and convinced me that I could make the short trek by myself. When it was my turn to go, he just pointed to a small hole in the line of trees and said, "Just walk that way and follow the trail. There are a couple of them but you will figure it out."

So I took a deep breath, said a little prayer that my inner fearless mountain girl would rise to the challenge, and ventured into the woods. My little lantern did not shine ahead; instead it only lit my steps as I took them. Faced with a wall of trees and two path options (neither of which I could see into beyond the first step) and a chorus of too-close and too-strange animal noises, I confidently turned on my heels and walked back to camp, where I demanded that Nathan drive me to the bathhouse himself. Turns out that I have no inner fearless mountain girl, just a very small and demanding bladder. I would wait to learn the path in the daylight, when I could see further than one step ahead.

I would like to think that I am not a control freak. That I can roll with the punches. That things do not have to go my way or be done my way in order for me to find satisfaction. I have never been one of those mothers who thought there was only one way to change a diaper or give a baby a bath. I was happy to walk out the door for a dinner date with my gal pals, leaving my husband to raise his children however he saw fit. I didn't care how (or *if*, truth be told) the kids got clean, as long as I wasn't doing the changing or the bathing. And I was *not* about to call and check in; that would be asking for trouble. If he needed me he would call; otherwise, I was out of sight and off-duty. I listened with curiosity to my friends who could spend the entire dinner complaining about the way their husbands packed a diaper bag or mixed up rice cereal. Why did they care? I would sit and nod, silently guessing that if their husbands were smart, they would eventually just do things poorly in order to get off the hook, or perhaps they would just stop helping altogether. Who wants to help someone who keeps telling you that you are doing it the wrong way? I personally liked the help with the kids, and who was to say that my way was best anyway? Me, a control freak? Nope, no way.

My husband likes rivers, forest, mountains, and surprises. I like lakes, pastures, valleys, and wish lists. I like to be able to see what is ahead and plan accordingly. Long ago I accepted that life was always going to throw me curveballs. I accepted the reality that I am not in charge; I cannot control what other people do or say or think. I know that I don't have to control what is next, but I want to be able to control my reaction, and I want to be prepared for all contingencies. I like to see what is on even the most distant horizon no matter what it is. No matter how bad or how wonderful.

Maybe this is why I like lakes and valleys and pastures. I can see all there is to see. I can stand in one place and look from side to side to see what is coming, what is ahead, what is behind. Rivers, woods, and mountains make me nervous with their sharp turns, bends you cannot see around, narrow paths that seem to never end, overgrown brush that grabs from every direction, strange animals ready to pounce and hiding in tree stumps. That night in the woods, desperately needing to find a bathroom but completely frozen in my tracks, I had to admit that perhaps I am more of a control freak than I like to admit. Sure I can roll with the punches—as long as I see the punch coming. Yes, I adapt well to change—as long as I can see the change taking form and make my plans accordingly. I may not demand that life go according to my plans, but I tend to demand that life give me a chance to adjust my plans.

I know I do this with God, too. I don't try to tell God what to do specifically, but I do give him multiple-choice options. I say things like "Okay, God, if we are going to have to move I would like to move here, here, or here," and I call that being open to God's will. I call that not being a control freak. "See, God," I say, "I am totally open to all these options." And then I smile my cutest smile, hoping he will overlook the fact that I have narrowed his choices and go along with one of my plans. I think perhaps instead of a multiple-choice test, what God wants from me is something more like a blue book. Remember the blue books in college? For the really big finals that were all essay questions? Instead of a bubble sheet, with choices *A* through *D,* God asks us to hand him a blank blue book, saying to him, "Here, you write the story."

St. Stephen is the first known martyred disciple, one of the first seven deacons appointed by the apostles. I am pretty sure martyrdom will never be on my multiple-choice list. And perhaps it wasn't on Stephen's either. But when I read Stephen's words in Acts 6 and 7, his retelling of the story of the Jewish people, I see example after example of people who set out to do things their way, even things they thought they were doing for the Lord, only to have him intervene, and change the plans, to tell the story a different way. As Stephen tells the stories of Moses, Abraham, and Joseph, he points out how through history men have tried to stifle and stop God's plan because it was too wild, too unpredictable, and too strange. How even good men, religious men, have throughout valued control over faith, the manageable over the blank, empty pages of a blue book. The truth of this speech was too much for those men listening to bear, too wild, too radical. Stephen, so full of faith, the glory of God on him so heavily that his face shown like an angel, was an assault on the men who had challenged him. His words and his presence called into question their character, their belief system, their entire way of living, and it was more than they could take. So to silence their fears they stoned Stephen to death.

Now, all these years later, the day after the most lushly celebrated day in Christendom comes St. Stephen's feast day. By December 26, Christ has been born, hope has come, and we know all will be well. But on St. Stephen's Day, if we look up from our gifts, from our new gadgets and toys, if we turn off the television, and sit for just one minute in silence, perhaps we will be reminded that this is not a sweet, feel-good pageant we are watching. This is instead a wild, wonderful, and unpredictable life we have been called to. We must throw away our safe plans, our multiple-choice ideas of obedience, and hand our Creator and Master a very large and very blank blue book, and allow him to write the story he chooses for us, regardless of whether we know how to pack for the adventure.

Origami-Inspired Twelve Days of Christmas Box Garland

I have always loved the "Twelve Days of Christmas" song. All those ladies in their party frocks dancing. A funny partridge in a funny pear tree. (Do partridges even like pears?) But I had no idea what any of it meant. A few years ago I stumbled across a children's book that paired the twelve verses with twelve basics of Christianity. After digging around I learned that some people believe that the Twelve Days of Christmas was a way to teach Catholic children their catechism through symbolism and song. Whether or not this story is true history or modern folklore, the fact remains that you can easily pair each verse of this traditional Christmas tune with the most basic and fundamental Christian teachings.

Materials Needed

- Sheet music or scrapbook paper
- Glitter
- Baker's twine or string, 2 yards
- Large sewing needle with large eye
- Glue stick
- Craft or school glue
- Thin paintbrush
- Printer
- White paper
- Scissors
- 12 pearl-topped straight pins (optional)

Directions

Start by printing or copying your Twelve Days of Christmas images (in chapter 23).

Cut them out, staying fairly close to the edge, and set them aside.

Cut your sheet music or scrapbook paper into 12 6 x 6-inch squares.

Following the traditional star box origami folding pattern (you can find great instructions at Origami-Instructions.com), make 12 star boxes.

After your boxes are folded to your satisfaction, glue one printed image in the center of each star box. Make sure that your image lines up with your star points facing north, south, east, and west.

Next, using your thin paint brush, paint the edges of the square frame opening of your box.

Sprinkle with glitter and let dry.

After everything has dried, you can string your garland.

Thread your needle with the baker's twine, knotting one end.

Starting with Day 12, thread your twine through the east point of the star coming back out the west point of the same star. The twine should run along the back of your star box.

Pull the star to the end of your length of twine and repeat this process for the other 11 star boxes.

When you are finished your stars should run left to right in the proper Twelve Days of Christmas order.

Take your straight pins and pin closed the north and south points of each star. You will then unpin and reveal the contents of one star each day from December 25 to January 6.

Each day between December 26 and Epiphany, open one box, starting with the first one in the song—the Partridge in a Pear Tree. As you open the boxes, take a moment to explain the alternate meaning for each image (as listed below). As the week progresses play a memory game to see who can remember and sing not only each verse of the song but also what each verse symbolizes. By the end of Christmastide, all the star boxes will be open and the whole family will have memorized some of the most basic and important foundations of our faith. Want to go deeper? Work together as a family to memorize each of the lists that are mentioned (Ten Commandments, Apostles' names, twelve steps of the Creed, and so on). If you still have young children, start with some simple ones like Day 3 or Day 4 and then tackle one new list each Christmas as your children grow older.

Traditional Meanings
for each of the Twelve Days

A partridge in a pear tree: Jesus

Two turtle doves: The Old and New Testaments

Three French hens: Faith, hope, and love

Four calling birds: The four Gospels

Five gold rings: The Torah/Pentateuch, first five books of the Old
Testament

Six geese a-laying: The six days of Creation

Seven swans a-swimming: Seven gifts of the Holy Spirit

Eight maids a-milking: Eight Beatitudes

Nine ladies dancing: Nine fruits of the Holy Spirit

Ten lords a-leaping: The Ten Commandments

Eleven pipers piping: The eleven faithful apostles

Twelve drummers drumming: Twelve points of the Apostles' Creed

Epiphany

The Feeling Guide

Before Happiness you are Adventurous.
You must be Adventurous to be Happy.
To be Determined you have to be Worried.
But it is hard to be Determined.
Mad is sometimes Worried.
If you are Mad you sometimes are Determined.
—Miles Greer, age seven

I have a habit of leaping before I look. Only I don't think of them as leaps. I just think of them as What Comes Next, but my sisters assure me that they are leaps, sometimes even big ones. My leaps aren't glamorous. They are not the sorts of leaps people make movies of. I haven't gone to Italy to eat pasta for three months or Bali to study with a medicine man (although I think both of those are great ideas for my life). I haven't rescued any orphaned children (yet), and I haven't moved to the middle of a gang-infested part of town, placing myself in the line of fire. I haven't become a missionary to a closed country. My leaps are much more domesticated.

45

EPIPHANY

Often my leaps are what I think Ann Voskamp meant in *One Thousand Gifts* when she said, "Sometimes you don't know when you're taking the first step through a door until you're already inside." I often don't realize what a chance I have taken until I am safely on the other side looking over the canyon I just crossed by tightrope. Leaps such as going to work as a nanny at the age of fifteen for three months, two thousand miles across the country from my family. Leaps such as getting married at twenty-two, buying a house at twenty-five, and having two babies before I was thirty. Leaps such as starting my own business, becoming a pastor, writing a book. Leaps such as taking jobs because they were the ones presented to me. I needed a job, there was a job, and I took it. Had I any experience that qualified me? Very little. Did that deter me? Never. I would learn, adjust, adapt.

This philosophy is how I have learned to cook over the years. My husband is a very recipe-following type of fella. I am more of a look-and-see-what-we-have-on-hand kind of gal. For the most part these leaps of culinary risk have paid off, but there has been the occasional flop. The bread that I set on fire, the rice that was crunchy, the eggs hard as hockey pucks. But then there are the recipes that turn out so yummy they will make you weak in the knees, and all the flops, all the failures, all the risk are worth it, because when you hit gold in the kitchen it can heal almost anything that ails you.

Despite the two boy Cabbage Patch knockoff dolls I had loved and raised as a little girl, by the time I was pregnant with my first child I was daydreaming of a family that looked like something from a Jane Austin novel, a Bennett-size gaggle of girls. Having been raised in a family that was happily overrun with womenfolk, I expected to continue the tradition. I dreamed of sharing all the things I loved best in a loud, joyful home filled with daughters. I fantasized about unveiling the kindred spirits of Anne of Green Gables and Audrey Hepburn to them, trading sparkling shoes when they grew, and obsessing about all things British over afternoon tea parties. When that first ultrasound revealed a little Gilbert instead of a little Anne, my shock was immediate and briefly disorienting. But soon I found my bearings and adjusted to the idea. Wylie was only my first child, after all; there would be chances for girls later on, lots and lots of girls. And so I transitioned into the idea of being a momma to one little boy and embraced all things Cowboy and Baseball, and I filed my girl names away with the vintage baby girl dresses I had picked up at flea markets and the cute little embroidered quilt topper featuring Mary and her little lamb.

I wish with all my might that I could say the second time I heard the words "It's a boy" I was not so shocked, my eyes were not like a jammed water gun suddenly released, an uncontrollable burst of hot liquid squirting from my eyes. That I didn't turn my head away from Wylie and Nathan to wipe away the evidence that my heart had just plummeted to the floor of that exam room.

I love my boys more than anything. They are amazing and beautiful. Smart, charming, and funnier than any other two people I have met, and my life is so much richer and beautiful because they are in it. I would not trade them for all the girls in the world, not even for Anne Shirley herself. But despite all of this, the truth will always be that they, my sweet wonderful boys, were not the adventure I had envisioned, and to deny that fact would be to live dishonestly, to sugarcoat my story, and what good would that do any of us?

Eventually I would move from shock at the unexpected to mourning what was not to be to acceptance and joy in what was. After all, I was never upset about what was. It was only what couldn't be that brought forth the tears. And so becoming a mother to only boys began stripping the illusion that I had any real control over the trajectory of my life.

EPIPHANY

What I had expected was a home full of girls, and what I got instead was a house full of boys. And the only control, the only smidgen of power I had in the whole deal, was how I would respond. I had my own little epiphany—I was the mother of boys. Boys. Boys who like dirt and sticks and slingshots. Boys who catch toads and bring them to the dinner table. Boys who want to take all my jewelry and bury it in the backyard, as all good pirates do with their loot.

How was I, a girly-girl, going to create a full, imaginative, and creative life with boys? I could only think of one answer: Adventure. I was going to have to create some adventures for them. I had leapt feet first into motherhood, and the result was boys. Now I was going to have to step out of my lovely, leisurely, indoor, ruffled-edged life and learn how to parent these wild, messy, active creatures according to who they were, not who I had thought they would be.

Sure, we would still have tea parties from time to time, in between their *Star Wars* versus *The Pirates of the Caribbean* battles, and gratefully both my boys are big readers and fans of imaginative play; they have been known to go to church in full Jack Sparrow garb, to the grocery store as Darth Vader, and to school in my trench coat while working on a case as Junior Detective. Both my boys have hearts as big as the ocean. They are sweet and kindhearted (except when they are fighting between themselves) and creative beyond measure (my walls bear the proof). But as they grow older, I have realized that they need me to do more than just watch, more than just pat them on the head as they run outdoors. They need me to jump in, participate, enter their world, and see it from their eyes. So I have learned how to pick up bugs, how to sword fight, how to give noogies, how to float the Buffalo River, how to cut an earthworm in half with my thumb nail so that both boys could have bait on their fishing poles, and how to hunt for Christmas trees.

In the fifteen years of our marriage, Nathan and I have had a variety of trees. We have bought fresh trees from the McAlpine Christmas Tree Farm in his small hometown country community, and we have bought them from the man sleeping in a camper in the K-Mart parking lot. We have put up fake trees handed down from my mother-in-law, which I attempted to flock myself with spray-on snow. There was our wonderful, white, metal outdoor tree we used indoors and the vintage tree that was so old it was more the color of yellow snow than white. But even though I loved or at the very least tolerated these trees, none of them ever seemed right. They were too full, too tame, too lush, too stiff. To me Christmas is none of these things. Christmas is bare, wild, and a little forlorn. Or at least that's how it feels to me. To me the tree is the most symbolic of all our decorations, and I wanted our tree to be as wistful and stripped bare on the outside as I felt on the inside. Why should our trees pretend to be something we are not?

This is how our annual Tree Hunt began the year Miles was two and Wylie was six. Anxious for the most perfectly imperfect *Charlie Brown Christmas Special* tree we could find, and bolstered by the conviction that my boys needed a greater connection to our family Christmas experience than opening a box full of plastic greenery or visiting a parking lot with farm-grown trees could provide, we set out on our first hunt. In those days my in-laws still lived in the country, and after Thanksgiving dinner we set out to find a nice, tall, wispy, pitiful tree that needed to be loved. It didn't take long before we found just that tree. While Nathan prepared to chop down our tree, the boys and I stood back, yelling "Timberrr!" at the top of our lungs. The next year my in-laws left the country for the city and we moved the hunt to my grandparents' property, where the adventure has continued for several years.

Sitting under this year's tree, in the final days of Christmastide, I cannot help but wonder if this will be our last city Christmas. For months now, our farm-life dreams have grown more vivid each day. As the boys have grown, as our lives have changed, there is a new adventure that has caught our hearts—that of life in the country, life on a small farm. This year, as I get ready to undress my tree, I imagine next Christmas. Will it be on a farm? Will the boys go into the woods on our own property to find us a tree? Am I ready for this next adventure? What if farm life is not what I expect it to be? Just because I am older, am I wiser? Am I any less at risk of being duped by my own heart? Am I willing to take the risk that it might not all go as I hope? If things turn out differently from what I expect (as they generally in some way do) and God presents me with a new plan, will I trust his goodness enough to say to him honestly "I don't like the plan" and then adjust and move on and follow his lead? Letting go of what I thought I wanted in order to embrace and love what I have?

Only occasionally is it lost on me that I am not just raising boys, but I am also raising men. I want to raise men who do not shy away from adventure, who are resilient, who can roll with the changes and the hurdles that living life on Planet Earth brings. I want to raise men who can say "I don't like the plan" but who do not stop there. I pray that they will also be able to say, "All right, God, what's next then?" I want to raise men who love God's ways more than their ways, and in order to do that I must live that sort of life as well. Just a few years ago wanting to move to the country was the furthest thing from my mind. I would never have dreamed of wanting to farm, to raise chickens and goats, to live miles from friends, Starbucks, and Target. But here we are. I have reached that place, thanks in large part to my boys. They made me a mother, and they have taught me that there is joy to be found in adventure. Thanks to them I am more willing to try new things and go places I would never have considered going before. I see the world differently, and I see my place in it differently as well.

There are certain days that I am more a mother than others. Days when I feel connected to the great task of mothering as a whole. When I feel a kinship with all the other mothers in the world, when I feel particularly close to the sisterhood, when the great responsibility of motherhood is palpable, and when I am more aware of the way one mother can affect a whole society than others. Inevitably in these moments I think of Mary. Epiphany to me is one of those days. Motherhood is an adventure and motherhood of the Messiah even more so. Epiphany is the day that I take down all my Christmas decorations, when all the fancy and folly of childhood—because Christmas is the one time we are all allowed to be six years old again—is packed up and the grown-up responsibilities of New Year's resolutions, filing our taxes, going back to work, and getting through the cold, dark winter months are what lie ahead.

Perhaps because of all of this I feel most like a mother on this January 6. To do all of these things is to choose to be a grown-up. To put aside the things I might rather be doing for the things that I need to do for the livelihood of my family, to be a responsible citizen of my country, to take care of what needs to be taken care of for the benefit of the whole. But all of this does not always come easily or naturally. I must be determined. I must have a spirit of tenacity. I must roll myself out of bed while the sun is still sleeping and begin my day, a day very similar to the dozen or so before this one, because it is what is needed. I have to think that Mary was this kind of mother as well.

I tend to see Mary more as being like the character portrayed by Imogene Herdmen in Barbara Robinson's book *The Best Christmas Pageant Ever*, "sort of nervous and bewildered, but ready to clobber anyone who laid a hand on her baby." I love that idea of Mary. So much more real than the serene, pink-cheeked, meek image we all have grown accustomed to seeing. So much closer to my experience of motherhood.

Mary didn't plan on becoming the mother of the Messiah any more than I planned on becoming the mother of two rowdy boys. She certainly did not spend her girlhood dreaming of being pregnant at her wedding, or giving birth in a barn, or having to flee the jealous rage of a madman all the way into another country. And I am pretty sure that she never envisioned three wise men, three Gentiles, showing up on camels at her doorstep, because of that pesky star that would not leave her alone. But there they were, all with their gifts. Fulfilling the prophecies, declaring her boy child to be the Savior for the world. Perhaps it was at this moment that Mary realized just what she was in for, that all her preconceived ideas of family life may have to be thrown out with the bathwater. At that moment there was no going back, no pretending that things were going to be "normal now." As far as I can tell, Mary did what all good mothers do. She did what she had to do; she kept her child safe for as long as she could, she looked for him when he was lost, she chided him to be helpful, encouraged him out of the nest, and when it was time, despite her own wants, she let him go.

As I take down my Christmas, packing up all the tinsel and all the bows, as I get us ready to go back to work and school, putting in the laundry, making sure we all have clean underwear, as I tell my boys to do their chores and to clean up their Legos, as I transfer the money from savings to checking to pay for the third pair of eyeglasses in one year, I think of Mary. Pain changes the status quo. Ah, yes. And so does motherhood.

Packing-up-the-Tree Party

If you are like me, taking down the Christmas tree is not nearly as much fun as putting it up but, boy, does it come down faster than it goes up. The holidays can be so busy that I don't always get to visit with everyone as much as I would like. Who says that the fun has to end on December 25 or even January 1? Officially, according to the church calendar, Christmastide is not over until January 6, so on Epiphany invite your friends over to help you un-decorate, tempting them with a gourmet sandwich bar and rewarding them with ice cream floats. Before you know it, all your Christmas splendor will be stored away till next year.

Tips To have a fun (and productive) Un-Decorating Party

1. Have a plan—organize a to-do list by sections (the tree, the mantel, the dining room, and so on) that includes specific tasks.
2. Form teams—assign guests to a team, grouping smaller helpers with bigger ones. Think about who is better at wrapping delicate ornaments and who might be better at lifting heavy boxes.
3. Have bins and packing items ready—in each room have your boxes, leftover wrapping and tissue paper, and bubble wrap set out, ready and waiting.
4. Have a party contest—which team can finish first? Which team breaks the fewest items? Who is the most organized?
5. Send guests home with a goody bag—before your party, hit up post-Christmas sales for discounted ornaments and let each guest choose one for his or her own as a thank-you treat. Let each guest make a brown bag lunch for the next day from the leftover sandwich fixings.

Sweet Man's Cold Cut Sandwiches for a Crowd

When I was growing up, a sandwich was just a sandwich. A piece of meat slapped between two lackluster pieces of bread. That all changed when I married Nathan. The man can build a sandwich. Here are a few tips from him on how to make the best sandwiches on the block.

Sandwich Bar

Select two or three items from each category, depending on what you and your family like on a sandwich. Set all of the items up on a buffet near a toaster or oven with the broiler on low.

Sliced deli meats

Sliced charcuterie

Sliced cheese

Vegetables

Pickles

Dressings

Breads

Seasonings

Sides such as potato salad, chips and dip, or baked beans

Tips for a superb sandwich

- Lightly toasting the bread will prevent the sandwich from becoming soggy.
- Try to avoid putting slick flat layers together in the sandwich (for example, meat and cheese with dressings). This will prevent items from shooting out the back of your sandwich when you squeeze it to get it in your mouth. I prefer to always fold my cold cuts over instead of laying them flat for the same reason.
- Mustard goes best against the bread. Salad dressing or mayonnaise goes best with the vegetable layer. There is no law that says you cannot put mustard on both slices of bread and smear your mayo right onto the lettuce or sprouts.
- If you are going to put dry seasonings on your sandwich, put them on a damp layer, such as the tomato slices.
- Before eating, always place toothpicks in the sandwich and carefully cut it in half with a very sharp serrated knife. Again, this makes it much easier to eat without its falling apart.
- If your sandwich is any good, it will drip. Lean over a plate and have a good cloth napkin or dish towel handy.

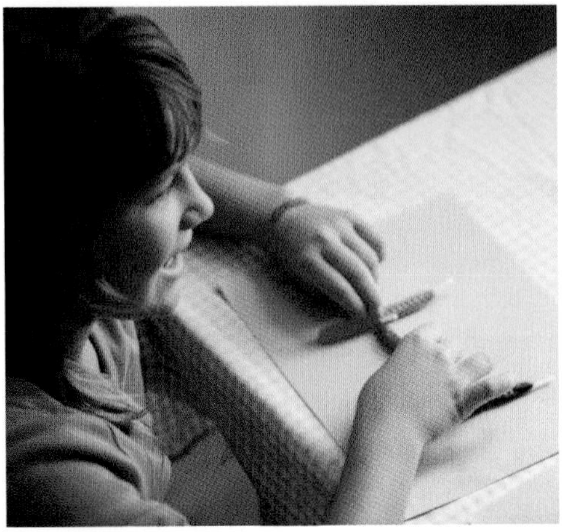

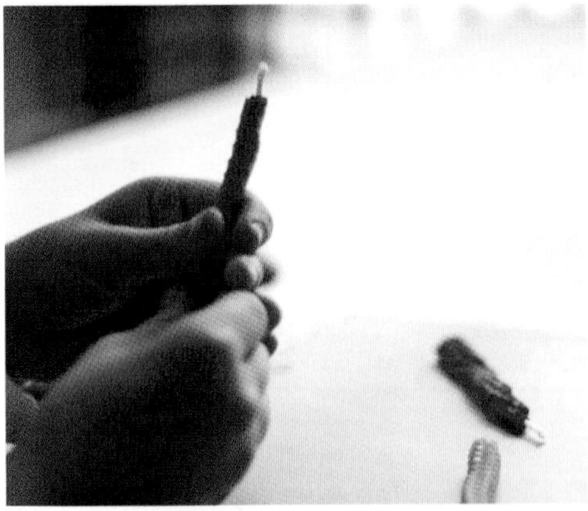

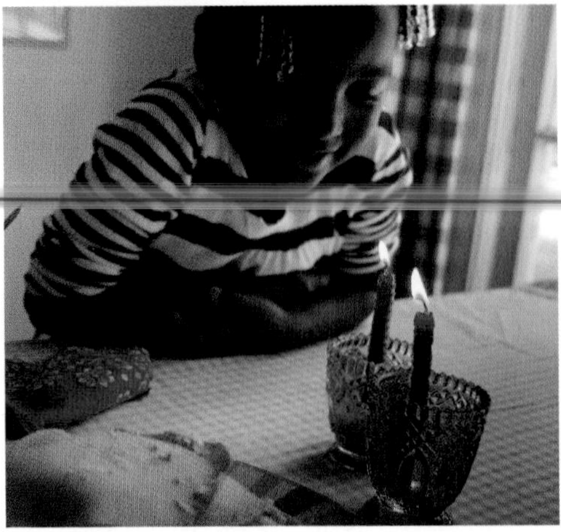

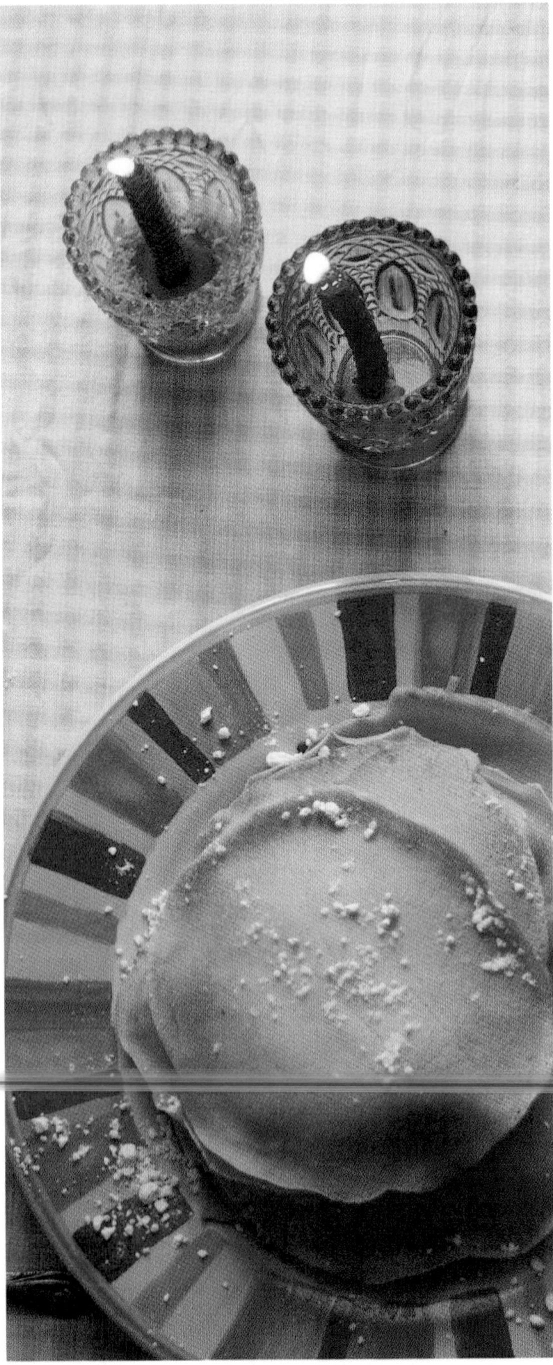

chapter 6

Candlemas

February 2

> Learning to live in the present moment is part of the path of joy.
> —Sarah Ban Breathnach,
> *Simple Abundance*

When I was twelve, my family moved from Clearwater, Florida, to Juneau, Alaska, where I lived until I left for college. There was no better match for my angst-filled adolescence than a place where gloom and doom, rain and fog, snow and dark skies dominated the calendar. Of course, the dreary days were punctuated by occasional golden days that appeared in late spring and early summer. Those are the days you see on the cruise ship commercials—there are about five of them all year. I now live in the South, where the opposite weather patterns prevail. I reside in a land where they have actually closed school at the mere threat of snow, before a single flurry has even fallen from the blessed sky.

But that cold, dark, and sullen weather of Southeast Alaska that so perfectly matched my deep, poetic thirteen-year-old soul did not hold the same attraction for my stay-at-home mother of four. Our house in Juneau had three walls of picture windows in the family room that looked out over Gastineau Channel and the high-

57

CANDLEMAS

way bridge that ran across it. In those first few months after our move to Juneau, my mother would stand at those windows, staring out at the constant rain, at the smothering gray that surrounded her on all sides in the daytime, and the deep, cold, black that seeped in when the sun, which had never really come up at all, finally went down. At the time, I thought she just liked to look at the mountains and the water. I now know that she was making her peace with raising a large, rambunctious family in a place where you could only really play outdoors two months out of the year.

On the deepest winter mornings before school, the sky was so heavy and dark that I could not even see the ground right below our windows—only the lights on the highway and on top of the snowplows and school buses that blinked without ceasing. There was never a reason to turn on the TV to see if work and school had been canceled due to a particularly heavy snowstorm. All we needed to do was peer out those picture windows and look for the blinking lights to know all was well. Life would continue as it had the day before.

The celebration of Candlemas reminds me of those mornings. As those in the Roman Catholic faith well know, Candlemas is the official end of Christmas for the Western world. This is the day that has been marked to remember when Jesus was presented at the temple as an infant by Mary and Joseph. Once in the temple, Jesus was blessed by the prayer of Simeon, in the presence of Anna the prophetess. Simeon, upon seeing the Messiah, gave thanks to the Lord, saying,

Sovereign Lord, now let your servant die in peace,
   as you have promised.
I have seen your salvation,
   which you have prepared for all people.
He is a light to reveal God to the nations,
   and he is the glory of your people Israel! (Luke 2:29–33, NLT)

The tradition of blessing the beeswax candles began during what was termed the Candle Mass, when the priest would bless parishioners' candles and celebrate the presentation of Christ at the temple for the first time. The lighting and blessing of the candles is a way to draw inspiration from those words of Simeon, "He is a light to reveal God to the nations."

By the time February 2 rolls around, there is very little evidence of Christmas left at my house. The decorations have been packed up and stored for another year, the presents have lost their sheen (and often several parts), and I am back to eating salads and counting calories instead of enjoying homemade cookies and cakes morning, noon, and night.

In the mornings, I rise before my family, make breakfast, drink my coffee. My toes are cold. I stare out the back window at the lonesome patio furniture and forgotten toys waiting under the bare trees for spring's arrival. Winter is still here, bleak and bare, long outlasting the holiday finery that it arrived in. The initial romance of short days and long nights is beginning to wear thin. I stare at the frozen sky and wonder, *How much longer?* I think about my mother, staring out those windows, wondering what was ahead for her in the cold and frozen land she found herself in. I think about Mary, about how soon after she dedicated Jesus at the temple she had to flee to Egypt, completely unaware of what life held for her there.

Candlemas comes to me then, in those moments of wondering and cold toes. It comes full of light and warmth, it comes with beeswax candles and cups of steaming hot cocoa, signaling like those blinking lights on the snow plows and school buses, reminding me that Christmas was not a dream. Christ did come, and he is among us still.

Beeswax Candle Craft

Whether or not you attend a church gathering that blesses beeswax candles on Candlemas, you can still honor this tradition by making your own beeswax candles at home. Use them throughout the winter months to bring light into your home, save them for future unordinary day events, or give them as gifts.

When we decided to try this craft at home, I had a little bit of difficulty finding the supplies locally and eventually found them online through Etsy.com and Amazon.com. If you do not live in an area where these supplies are readily available, you may also want to purchase supplies online, in which case you should plan to order them a few weeks in advance so you have everything by February 2.

Materials Needed

- 2 x 4-inch sheets of beeswax in honeycomb pattern (1 per candle)
- Natural fiber wick (you will need a 4½-inch length for each candle)
- Hair dryer
- Scissors
- Smooth rolling surface (I created an easy-to-clean work surface by using the matte side of a sheet of freezer paper for each child)

Directions

Cut fiber wick into 4½-inch strips.

Place sheet of beeswax on smooth surface.

Heat with hair dryer to soften wax, 10–20 seconds on warm/low setting.

Once wax starts to feel soft and sticky, turn hair dryer off and immediately place wick on wax, lengthwise, toward one edge, and press wick into wax.

When the wick is secure, begin rolling the wax around the wick, until you have rolled the sheet into a taper.

To make larger candles, simply purchase larger sheets and more wick and repeat the process.

Mrs. Jackson's Hot Cocoa

In Mexico, Candlemas is called Día de la Candelaria and is celebrated by feasting on homemade tamales and drinking hot chocolate.

Since I was a little girl, my mother has made the most wonderful hot chocolate mix, and to this day I can still lure friends over for a visit with the promise of a hot cup of Mrs. Jackson's Cocoa. The recipe will make quite a bit of cocoa, as Mrs. Jackson loves to give jars of it away as gifts throughout the winter months. The mix will stay fresh for many months if stored in an airtight container.

Directions

In a very large bowl, mix together the following ingredients:

2   25.6-ounce boxes of nonfat dry milk

1   16-ounce jar of nondairy creamer

3   16-ounce cans of quick chocolate drink mix

2   8-ounce cans of Hershey's unsweetened cocoa

1   2-pound bag of confectioners' sugar

Mix all together and store in an airtight container.

To serve in a standard 8-ounce mug: Measure 1/3 cup of the mix into mug, fill with hot water, stirring thoroughly for a few seconds.

Top with fresh whipped cream and sprinkles.

(You may not find these items packaged in these exact amounts. Use a measuring cup or weight scale to get the amounts you need.)

Candlemas Crepes

In France, Candlemas is called La Chandeleur and crepes are the food du jour. There is a French legend that if you hold a lucky coin in one hand and flip your crepe in the pan in the other hand without dropping the crepe, then you will have a prosperous year. Whether this has ever been proven I cannot say, but it would be a fun challenge.

Ingredients

2   cups flour

3   eggs

¼   teaspoon salt (I love fine sea salt for this recipe)

1   tablespoon sunflower oil

2   cups plus 1 tablespoon whole milk

Directions

Mix ingredients together in a blender; mixture will be very thin. Cook these in a non-stick skillet or a crepe pan that has been lightly greased, on medium heat.

Crepes can be served as a savory or sweet dish, depending on how you fill or top them. My favorite crepes are filled with a creamy chicken mixture and served over a bed of sticky rice.

For Candlemas, try creating a "crepe bar" by putting out lots of different fillings and toppings. Let each person create his or her own unique savory or sweet crepe dinner.

Some filling ideas for the crepe bar are:
Ricotta cheese
Shredded cheese
Plain or vanilla yogurt
Fresh fruit, sliced thinly
Shredded chicken
Sautéed mushrooms
Sour cream
Maple syrup
Nutella® spread
Butter
Powdered sugar
Fruit jam

63

Spring

Lent

L iberate
E xpectations
n ourish
T hankfulness

hope

Shrove Tuesday

The Tuesday Before Lent

> Grace strikes us when we are in great pain and restlessness......Sometimes at that moment a wave of light breaks into our darkness, and it is as though a voice were saying, "You are accepted."
>
> —Paul Tillich,
> *The Shaking of the Foundations*

chapter 7

Confession: Before the age of twelve, I don't remember wanting to grow up and be anything other than a teenager. Sure, there was a brief stint when I fancied myself a gymnast, the next Mary Lou Retton, but that was a brief interlude in the one ambition that motivated all others: to be a teen. We can thank Liesl Von Trapp, immortalized as the I-am-sixteen-going-on-seventeen lass from the Julie Andrews version of *The Sound of Music*, for my obsession. Something about the song "Sixteen Going on Seventeen" embedded into my little-girl heart that there was nothing more wonderful on earth than being a teenager. I can remember requiring Maw to pick this tune out on the piano repeatedly so that I could croon it at the top of my six-year-old lungs.

This belief that the teen years were the most glorious of all years was solidified by my second obsession: *Joanie Loves Chachi*. Oh, yes, in my first-grade mind there had never been a romance as wild and wonderful as the one between Joanie Cunningham

67

SHROVE TUESDAY

and Chachi Arcola, and the fact that they were mere teenagers was icing on the cake. When other little girls were playing princess or mommy, I was playing High School Girl. When other little girls were pretending to turn their rooms into their palaces or kitchens, I was turning mine into what I imagined to be a dream teenager room. The pièce de résistance was an old, disconnected telephone where my imaginary boyfriends would call me up, and I would torture them with my flighty indecision and callous ways. Just like Joanie.

I had great confidence that my teenage years would result in me looking less like myself (short, pudgy, cowlick-y, gap-toothed) and more like Justine Bateman as Mallory on *Family Ties*—fashionable and chic—or Brooke Shields—tall in stature, tumbling luscious locks, perfect complexion, well-endowed, and thin. Very thin. Looking back, I realize now that I really thought I would turn into my mother, who was all those things and more. Needless to say, my teenage years were not all I had dreamed they would be. A miraculous change of DNA did not occur and instead of a TV teenage queen, I was an only slightly taller, frizzier-haired, blotchier-skinned, not thin, flat-chested version of my younger self. I should have learned then that there is no point in counting chickens before they hatch.

Confession: Having kids did not fix me. I was not somehow more whole, less botched-up, or more certain just because I had a kid. I had thought becoming a mother would be the magic solution, provide me with the missing piece. The hole in my life, in my heart, would finally be filled. I thought having a baby would result in all the stars aligning and my world finally making sense. I wouldn't be restless anymore. I would feel satisfied, happy, and full of purpose. I put all my eggs into that basket; I trusted the arrival of a baby and the title of mother to do those things and more. But what I found out was that, instead of it fixing me, I was still me, with all my holes and problems and questions—only now I was also exhausted and had a lot more laundry to do.

Confession: I am addicted to things that cost a dollar. I didn't vote in the last presidential election, and I prefer bleached and processed pasta. I am pridefully protective of the first, I am arrogant in my neglectfulness in the second, and I am apologetic of the third.

Confession: I haven't loved my neighbor as I love myself. I have had a snarky tone, a judgmental heart, and a condescending attitude toward people who I think should know better. I avoid pain by hiding behind busyness. I put my wants above those in need, abusing and taking advantage of the airline instruction that one should put on one's own oxygen mask first. I am stingy and do not give freely. I am as full as a hot air balloon.

It is Shrove Tuesday or Shrovetide (or "Fat Tuesday," as some around here like to call it), the day before Ash Wednesday. The term *shrove* comes from the old English word *shrive*, which means to confess all sins. And on this day, this eve of Lent, that is what I am doing: I am confessing the silly, the ridiculous, the humbling, and the shameful. I am confessing my sins, my bad attitudes, my secrets. Confession means different things to different people. I didn't grow up in a tradition that practiced confession corporately or really practiced it all. To me, confessing was something you did only if you got caught, or if you were a glutton for punishment.

I was in my early twenties with a newborn baby, a husband, and a mortgage. It wasn't until then that the words "Confess your sins to each other and pray for each other so that you can live together whole and healed" (James 5:16) snapped into place in my heart. I made my first confession, waiting for a table at a burger joint. I confessed then to my friend, sitting on the stool beside me, that having a baby had not fixed me or my life. In fact, it had had quite the opposite effect. I had spent several years up to that point obnoxiously and arrogantly forcing my opinions of childbearing and rearing on others, including those in my church, whose children's ministry I ran. Because I believed that being a mother was the most noble of callings,

I could not imagine that it wouldn't bandage and heal all the parts of me that felt fractured, unraveled, wrong.

In those first few days at home with my sweet newborn boy, I would sit on the couch and stare at him in his bouncy seat, stunned at how I felt: exactly the same on the inside. Motherhood had failed to deliver wholeness to my heart in one swift move. It had delivered another layer of love, yes, I loved my son with my whole heart, but underneath there I was still: me, the same girl I had always been. The same confused, selfish, tired, rudderless girl.

That blunt statement to a friend held perhaps the first, most honest, humbling words I had said in my adult life up to that point. I didn't say them to gain her sympathy. I said them because it was the confession of my heart. It was pure truth, and I was so sleep-deprived that pure, raw, unflattering truth was all I had to offer. I had arrogantly propagated the notion for years that having children was the be-all and end-all to life. And yes, children are amazing and wonderful and life-changing. But they are not Christ. Even the most beautiful baby cannot, by its mere existence, do what only Christ can do. And in that moment I confessed that my formula for happiness had not worked. And in that confession came forgiveness and healing. Forgiveness for myself, forgiveness from my self-righteous attitudes and words. Forgiveness for stubbornly putting my hope in something of earth instead of something of heaven.

Healing came in the form of my friend's reaction, this friend whose own story included struggles with infertility issues, thanking me for my honest confession. It helped her know that even if she were to have a child someday, it would not fix her. It wasn't the miracle formula to fixing all the broken parts of her life either. She was released from the bondage that comes from chasing that which you are the most convinced will solve your problems and bind your wounds, instead of running head first into the arms of Christ.

In that moment, through the spilling out of those words, I understood how confession in the context of community is meant to heal, how it is meant to help us live full, authentic lives. How bringing out into the light the broken places and the failures and humble moments of raw truth should not diminish us in each other's eyes, not if we are walking in Christ's love. Instead, it should bring a sense of "Oh, you too? I thought I was the only one!"

I have found that when I cannot have grace for myself, if I confess my sins, my faults, my arrogance, my wrong thinking to those in my life who are walking in Christ's love and mercy, who show love to me as Christ does, just as I am, then they are able to pour the grace of God out on me, before I am even willing to pour out that grace to myself, and often I am able to return the gift. Those are the moments that create lasting community in my life. Those are what bring wholeness and redemption.

Breakfast for Dinner

Growing up in a Southern Baptist preacher's home meant church no fewer than three times a week, including Sunday nights. On Sundays our big meal was at noon, so Breakfast for Dinner became the evening tradition. We usually had scrambled eggs, a side of sausage or bacon, toast with butter, and homemade jellies. On occasion, pancakes or French toast made an appearance as well. When Nathan and I got married, we chose Breakfast for Dinner as the food for our reception, and now this tradition has become one of my kids' favorite meals as well. I was first introduced to the Dutch pancake when I visited a friend's farm in northwest Arkansas. I immediately thought of my boys and our Breakfast-for-Dinner tradition and could not wait to get home and create our own version together.

Iron Skillet Dutch Pancake with Whipped Lemon Cream

Ingredients for Pancake

3 tablespoons butter, at room temperature
4 large eggs
¾ cup milk
¾ cup all-purpose flour (make sure to level)
½ teaspoon sea salt
½ teaspoon pure vanilla extract
¼ cup sugar

Directions

Preheat the oven to 425 degrees.

Melt 3 tablespoons of butter in medium cast-iron skillet over medium heat; set aside.

Combine eggs, milk, flour, salt, cooled melted butter, vanilla, and sugar in a blender.

Blend well on high until mixture foams, about 1 minute.

Pour batter into the buttered skillet; bake until pancake is puffed and lightly browned, about 20 minutes.

The pancake will puff up and then fall as it cools.

While the pancake is cooking, whip together the topping.

Ingredients for Whipped Lemon Cream

1 package of instant lemon pudding mix
1 pint of whipping cream
   Juice of 1 lemon
   Rind of half of 1 lemon, zested
   Fresh raspberries

Pour the lemon juice and lemon pudding mix into a cold mixing bowl. (I usually stick mine in the freezer for a few minutes.) Slowly pour the whipping cream into the bowl, mixing on low at first, and then gradually increasing the speed until the mixture forms a thick spread. The consistency should be similar to that of whipped butter.

To serve, slice the Dutch pancake into eighths and serve with a large dollop of whipped lemon cream and a sprinkle of raspberries. This is a dish that is at its best while still warm.

Pancake Races

In Great Britain, pancake races are a Shrove Tuesday tradition. It is believed that pancakes came to be a part of Shrovetide because it was a way to use up all the eggs, butter, and milk, which were off limits during Lent. This race is a fun event for all ages: hold one in your neighborhood, at your church, or even in your kitchen with your kids.

Materials Needed

- 1 pancake for each team
- 1 plastic plate or a frying pan for each team member
- Starting line
- Finishing line

Divide everyone up evenly into teams. If you don't have enough people to do this as a relay, simply do it as a race.

Set your course. (For more challenge you can make it an obstacle course.)

The rules: each team member must run the course with the pancake in his pan or on his plate, flipping it continuously without it falling on the ground.

For a relay, the rule is that each runner must flip his or her pancake in the air and the teammate must catch the pancake in his or her pan or plate. The first team to have all members cross the finish line wins!

chapter 8

Ash Wednesday

The First Day of Lent, Forty Days Before Easter

"I try to believe," she said, "that God doesn't give you more than one little piece of the story at once. You know, the story of your life. Otherwise your heart would crack wider than you could handle. He only cracks it enough so you can still walk, like someone wearing a cast. But you've still got a crack running up your side, big enough for a sapling to grow out of. Only no one sees it. *Nobody sees it.* Everybody thinks you're one whole piece, and so they treat you maybe not so gentle as if they could see that crack."

—Rebecca Wells, *The Divine Secrets of the Ya-Ya Sisterhood*

I always buy corn on the cob in the husk. I can never resist it. Partially it is the price. Corn in the husk are a much better deal than those that have been already shucked, and I love a deal. Also, cobs fresh out of the husk just taste better. But mostly I buy it because I like the mess. I like the release of pulling the husk back. I love the ripping sound, the hard thrust of force that reveals the golden silks, so fine they are almost translucent, and the fresh corn kernels just underneath.

I have frozen ears of corn in their husks; I have forgotten them, pushed into the back of the refrigerator behind leftovers and gallons of milk and half-eaten containers of yogurt. But I have yet to leave any cob long enough in its husk for it to spoil. Despite the mutated appearance of the graying husk, the corn cob is well hidden inside, protected. All of its juicy kernels are still ripe, golden, and sweet.

When I begin to prepare the corn, the first thing I do is take our large cutting knife—butcher-like in its power—and I whack the tops of each corn husk off, careful to not cut the cob itself. I love the sound of the knife slicing and crashing through the husk, the hard *thwack* on the cutting board. Using the back of the knife, I sweep off the severed husk heads into a paper bag sitting on the chair beneath the lip of the counter. Each head falls to the bottom of the sack swiftly and quietly. Picking up the headless cob, I dig my thumb into the side of the sheath, peeling it swiftly back in one brash motion—this is not like peeling a banana, a task that requires a balanced, gentle, and patient hand. No, with a corn husk you must use more force, determination, and speed. I rip each section of husk back from the cob, pulling as many silky strands as I can at once, exposing the golden cob to the light of the evening sun, setting slowly, peering in my window, dancing across the counter. Later, as I read Ann Voskamp's words, "There is no seeing God face to face without first the ripping," I remember the corn and the satisfaction that comes with each swift, tearing motion. Yes. That is it. The ripping is what reveals.

I rinse off the naked cob in the sink, rub out as many of the stray silks from their hiding places as I can, working swiftly, with my fingers numb under the constant rush of icy tap water. I hear the water bubbling and popping on the stove, and I know it is ready. I drop each cob into the boiling pot of water. I leave them in just long enough for them to climb back to the surface, watch them roll a few times, fight for space against the boil, against each other. Using tongs that have seen better days, I quickly snap each one out of the pot, place them on the chipped serving platter that I love: the one with the aqua blue rim, spidery fractures running through its belly. I set the platter on the table, the last dish to be served, its timing pertinent to its enjoyment. We all use napkins to reach for the still steaming pieces; each of us rushes to bathe it in butter and sea salt before it cools. Our teeth break the golden skins and warm, sweet juices pour down our chins. We wipe them away with our wrists only to take another bite and another and another until we have stripped the cob bare. And then we move on to the meat and the salads and the French bread. These three could always wait. But the corn? The corn *had* to come first.

As we fill and refill our plates with the other bounty of our table, on each plate lies a solitary naked piece of corn, stripped bare and used up, bound for the compost pile along with its discarded husk, where they will be broken down beyond recognition and return again to the earth. Is this not what Ash Wednesday does for our hearts, souls, and minds? It strips them bare. Lays them naked. Broken down to our barest essence, we are the same as the ashes we encounter on this day; we are dependent on the gift of redemption, the transformation that comes from the process of dust to dust.

Ash Wednesday Bonfire

In many liturgical traditions Ash Wednesday is marked by a formal worship service or Mass in which the priest or church leader will make the sign of the cross out of a paste made of ash and sacramental oil on the foreheads of the congregants. Often the ashes are palm fronds that have been burned from the previous year's Palm Sunday service. The purpose of this service is to mark the beginning of the Lenten season of repentance and reflection. Because my church family is not a traditional liturgical community and does not hold annual Ash Wednesday services, we wanted a way for our family to participate and honor the common traditions that would still feel authentic and personal to us, and so the bonfire idea was born. Even though our gathering was centered on a city backyard fire, this is something that can be done on a bigger scale with a community around a large country bonfire or on a smaller scale around a group of candles or indoor fireplace. The point is not how grand you can make the occasion, but instead it is that you make time for the occasion in the first place.

Ash Wednesday Bonfire Activities

Burning of Confessions

Somewhere near your fire, perhaps on a small table, provide all those in attendance with pencil and paper and then prompt them to write down those things from their past that they would like to burn away, asking, "God, make a fresh start in me, shape a Genesis week from the chaos of my life" (Psalm 51:10). Then have everyone crumple up and toss their confessions into the fire, or put them on the end of a roasting stick and watch God burn up the old ashes returning to the earth, where something new will spring up.

Toasting Marshmallows

Everyone loves to make s'mores and toast marshmallows over an open fire! But have you ever watched a marshmallow burn to a crisp? A marshmallow that has been burned on the outside is still soft and white on the inside, so much softer than it was before. This is a great tactile example of how God uses the "refining fires" of life (various forms—pain, loss, change, love, and so on) to soften our hearts and loosen our grip on the illusion of control.

The Season

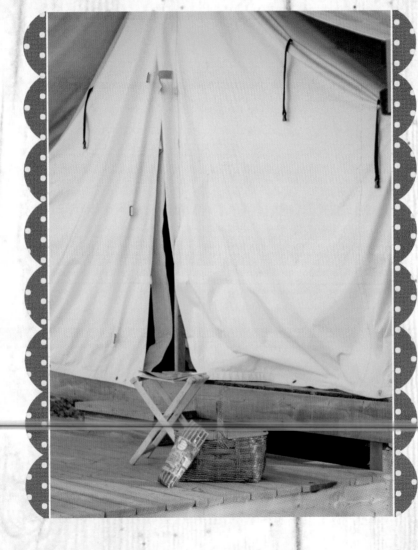

of *Lent*

> I've pitched my tent in the land of hope.
> —Acts 2:26

As the summer between my freshman and sophomore years at college rapidly approached, one picture painted itself over and over in my mind: that of me sitting on top of my suitcase on the curb of an abandoned university campus with nowhere to go. I needed a job, but not just any job. I needed a job that came with a place to live for the summer. The only logical move was to get a job working at a summer camp, where room and board were part of my payment. And so, at the wise old age of nineteen, I found myself a senior counselor at a Christian summer camp that was wildly popular with kids from all over the middle South, owing to its homespun charm. The camp's lack of bells and whistles was made up for with an abundance of fun, cheerfulness, and counselors who were as goofy as they were sincere.

One of the youngest and newest counselors, I had to pay my dues by leading some of the less interesting daily activities, such as paddle boats and relay races in the sweltering Arkansas heat. But by the second week of camp, I got my big chance to teach both of my dream classes, drama and journalism. I found my groove with the drama class quickly, leading the kids in some highly dramatized productions that were acted out to current praise and worship songs. Not exactly the stuff of Broadway, I know, but considering we had no stage, no budget, and four days to perfect each performance, I think they turned out pretty well.

On a following Monday morning, excited and full of optimism, I approached the weekly activity posting for counselors to find that, instead of journalism, I had been assigned the Nature Hut. I think I must have read that list twenty times trying to see if I had read it wrong. Me? The Nature Hut? I was the least "Mother Nature" person working at the camp. I had, in fact, spent the majority of my life up to that point declaring very loudly that I "didn't do" nature. But no sweet-talking or begging or pouting would get my boss to change my assignment. The Nature Hut was mine. So I had a choice. I could do a pitiful job and guarantee a week of misery for my campers and myself, or I could dig deep in the well of resourcefulness, say many, many prayers for help, and embrace the Nature Hut and all its glorious potential. I had to decide then and there where to pitch my tent.

The Nature Hut consisted of a lean-to shack, an impossibly old and lonely pony, some goats with questionable attitudes, and a family of turtles that I am pretty sure could have used a healthy dose of Prozac. I have found when teaching kids you must be confident in your ability to lead and in your knowledge of your subject, or you are toast. Kids can smell lack of preparation like a dog can smell bacon. And if by chance you aren't confident, you'd better be great at faking it. So at first I faked it. And then I learned it. And then I loved it. There were no Nature Hut lesson plans when I took over. There was no road forged for me. The only pictures I could study were the faces of my campers and the beauty of our surrounding campgrounds. I had to jump in and find my way with the barest of instructions and a whole lot of hope. I took on the cranky goats everyone else was afraid of, teaching the kids how to feed and care for them bravely and carefully. I organized Nature Trail Hikes that included a "how to" on making a hobo pack for the ultimate hiking experience, complete with sticks and handkerchiefs and a delicious trail mix we assembled ourselves with supplies I raided from the camp kitchen and counselor snack stash.

Together, the kids and I built turtle habitats and painted rocks and learned all about local insects and bugs and, most important, how to identify poison ivy. We went on hayrides and scavenger hunts, and we turned the Nature Hut from the underdog activity to one of the most popular that year. In a delightful twist of fate, my boss from that summer is now a great friend who attends our church. In fact, a few months ago I had the wonderful honor, as one of his pastors, of officiating at his wedding. I was pleasantly surprised to learn that he also remembered that summer of the Nature Hut, and how successful his risk and my resourcefulness turned out to be. God probably knew it all along, but I am glad I didn't. I am pretty sure it would have taken some of the magic out of the thing.

I didn't grow up experiencing the season of Lent, and over the years my practice of these sacred days has been informed by what I have read in books, by conversations with those who were raised practicing this tradition, by the Scriptures that inspired the formation of this season, and what I have observed, up close and at a distance. To me Lent is always about the desert. It is about Christ choosing to walk into the desert, setting up camp there, and then choosing to deny each temptation that was brought to him. Lent is also about the Israelites. I think of them choosing to leave Egypt, how they marched into the desert by choice. It was not the picture of freedom and glory they had imagined; they didn't expect forty years of eating manna and wandering in circles. These were not the images comforting them in those many years of captivity and not the dreams lulling them to sleep for eons of slavery. Even though they were in the desert for longer than they expected, God gave them the choice—the choice to adjust their attitudes, the choice to trust, to obey, to follow, to pitch their tents in the land of hope instead of the land of complaints and bitterness.

Every year, as I approach Lent, I think back to all the deserts that pockmark the map of my life, the little ridges they have left on my heart, like raindrops dried on a page, unshielded from storms. I think about where I staked my tent in those deserts. This year I've been reflecting on those deserts like my summer in the Nature Hut, those moments I had choices, big and little, when I opted for hope versus the times I opted for ingratitude. I cannot ignore the differences between the times I surrendered to trust and faith, and the times I fought with all my might, digging my heels in, refusing to budge my will and my heart. Guess which ones I bear the most scars from? And I think of the deserts yet to come—the ones I cannot even fathom, whose images I will not and cannot conjure in my imagination. Will I be able to give up and turn over to Christ those things that are hardest for me to let go? Those things to which I feel entitled? Those things I expect, whose pictures I have painted in my mind's eye? Will I choose—can I choose—to surrender those things that I lean on for comfort, instead of leaning on the One who gave up all comforts in order to give me the one thing I need most—Life? These are the questions that run through my heart like the tickertape headlines at the foot of the news channel as I enter into the desert of Lent and pitch my tent.

Camping Trip

The summer that I worked at the camp and taught in the Nature Hut was also the first summer I ever camped in a tent. I have found that although I do not think of myself as an outdoorsy girl, there are two areas related to nature that I do enjoy: farm life and camping, primarily because they are both highly domestic and filled with purpose. I love a nice hotel with room service as much as anyone. But there is something so lovely about camping, something so basic and freeing. It is real, it is authentic. If it rains, you get wet. If it is hot, you sweat. If it is cold, you shiver. You have to work hard to get camp set up. Everyone has to work together. Assignments are given: you help me with the tent, you gather wood for the fire, you unpack. You have to get along in tight spaces. Essentially camping requires effort, and to enjoy it you must choose to have a good attitude no matter what happens because, believe me, when you camp, anything can and will happen.

No matter where you live there are ways to camp year-round. Whether you rent a cabin, throw up a tent in the backyard, visit a state park and stay in a yurt, or simply turn off the lights and set up camp in your family room, you can find ways of unplugging from modern conveniences and gleaning what is best about doing things the "old-fashioned way" (as my boys would say), entering into Lent slowly and with great purpose.

Papaw's Toolbox Taters

When Nathan was growing up, his grandfather Papaw made these for him often. They are now the stuff of legends, and we eat them every time we go camping.

Ingredients

3 pounds red potatoes
2 large Vidalia onions
2 tablespoons butter
2 tablespoons vegetable oil
2 teaspoons salt

Directions

Wash potatoes thoroughly and cut out any bad spots, but leave peel on. Cut potatoes lengthwise and then slice into wedges. Peel onions and cut in half lengthwise, then cut into strips top to bottom. Heat vegetable oil and butter in a large cast-iron skillet over medium high heat on a camp stove. When the foam subsides, add the onions with half of the salt and cook until soft. Add in the potatoes and the rest of the salt. Cover with a sheet of foil. (To keep ours cooking without using up too much propane, we moved the covered skillet to the campfire, where we had placed a grill over some hot coals, and left it there to slow cook.) Turn the potatoes gently every 8 to 10 minutes until they are soft and done.

Lenten Sampler and Tote

Since the fifteenth century, sewing samplers have been used as a way to record, teach, and learn. Initially developed as a way for someone to record "a sample" of an interesting stitch, samplers were refined over time, and in the eighteenth and nineteenth centuries they were used to teach young women basic sewing techniques. Because of the attention required to sew a sampler, these domestic chores also served to teach young girls their numbers and the alphabet, as well as Bible verses, recipes, and other bits of household wisdom.

This Lenten Sampler follows that same purpose; it is a way to remember, to celebrate. This is one of those projects that may never be finished, or perhaps will take you several Lenten seasons to finish, as you create a visual and tactile record of the trials, the deserts, and the redemptive story of your own life. Here, you can record the joy, the tears, and the growth that have come as a result of those experiences.

For the Sampler

Materials Needed

- 1 embroidery hoop
- 1 piece of soft fabric—a nice linen, heavy cotton, or a vintage piece such as I used (you will need approximately 2 yards of 36-inch-wide fabric)
- Embroidery thread in a variety of colors (I typically use DMC cotton 6-strand embroidery floss)
- Embroidery or crewel needle
- Variety of bits and pieces (buttons, charms, ribbon, and fabric)
- Computer scanner or printer
- Computer transfer paper for embroidery purposes
- Template (as provided in chapter 23)

Directions

Choose your base fabric.

You will need approximately 2 yards

Wash, dry, and iron your fabric.

Cut your fabric in half. Now you should have 2 individual 1-square-yard pieces.

Using your computer transfer paper, transfer the two Lenten templates from chapter 23 onto your paper.

Then, following the directions on your transfer-paper package, iron the two templates onto your fabric, centering one design in the middle of each square of fabric.

Now you are ready to embroider.

Choose your threads. I used a variety of cotton (new and vintage) embroidery floss in yellow, cherry red, aqua, and lime green for this project.

Next, follow the stitch guidelines as indicated on the pattern in chapter 23.

For the Tote

My mother, my sister Jemimah, and my good friend Jeanetta are master seamstresses and helped me with every sewing project in this book. The one thing I have learned from them is this. When you are sewing, press, press, press. The iron, that is. The more you iron between steps, the better off you will be and the fewer mistakes you will have to rip out.

Materials Needed

- 3 tea towels (my towels were 19 x 25½ inches)
- Sewing machine
- Thread (the color of your tea towels and the color of the sampler)
- Iron
- Scissors

Directions

Wash, dry, and iron tea towels. This will prevent shrinkage and puckering in the future.

For the handles, cut one towel in half, lengthwise, so that you end up with two long rectangular pieces.

Fold each rectangular piece over 3 times resulting in 4 equal layers lengthwise, and press.

Topstitch along all 4 sides ½-inch from edge of each rectangle.

These are your straps. Set straps aside.

Next, cut out your samplers, leaving a 2-inch edge around all sides of each sampler. Set aside.

Lay out the next towel and fold in half widthwise, then press the folded edge with an iron to create a crease.

Lay this towel down, with creased fold on the left.

Center (from right to left) one sampler to each side of this towel and press, making sure to leave more room above it than below (so you can fold the top over later).

Pin bottom and right side of tea towel together.

Turn inside out, press, and stitch together along bottom and open side ½-inch from edge

You have now made Bag A. Set aside.

Take your last tea towel and fold in half widthwise, wrong sides together.

Stitch along the bottom and open side (right) ½-inch from edge.

You have now made Bag B.

Turn Bag A right side out and insert Bag B into Bag A, pushing the the corners of B into the corners of A and making sure that the fold of Bag B rests against the sewn edge of Bag A and vice versa.

Stitch A and B together around the top pre-hemmed edges (these will not match up perfectly).

Fold down top of lined bag to a desirable cuff length and press.

To attach your straps, pin and topstitch each end of 1 strap to the folded cuff about 1 inch from the edge. Repeat for second strap.

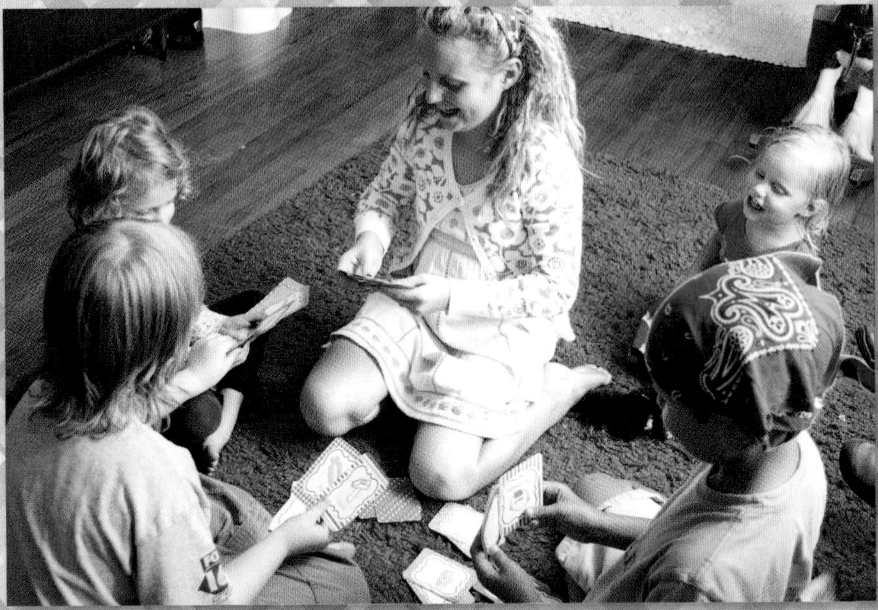

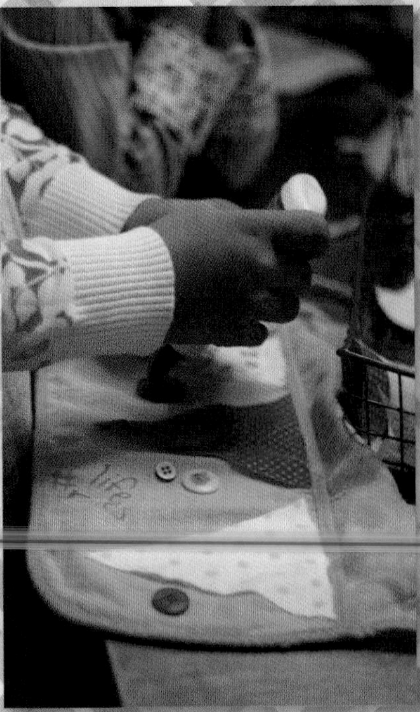

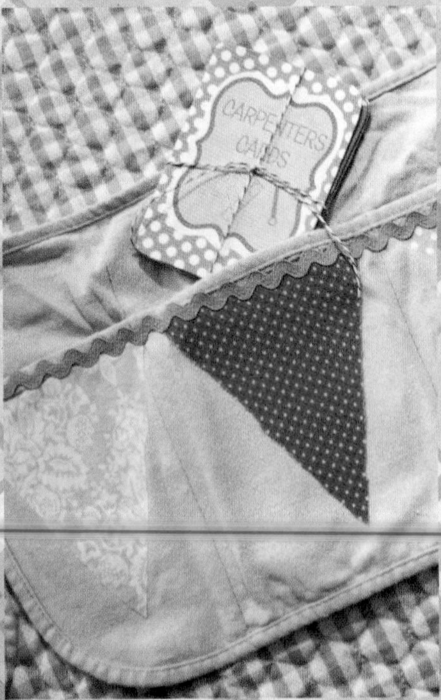
CARPENTERS
CARDS

chapter 10

St. Joseph's Day

> Only Christ could have brought us all together, in this place, doing such absurd but necessary things.
> —**Kathleen Norris**, *The Cloister Walk*

I am inside, clicking away on my laptop. The air conditioner is humming along, the weather unseasonably warm. I am nursing a cup of Community Dark Roast, with a splash of milk to cool it down. I fall into the "darker the better" camp of coffee drinkers. Somewhere, the boys are playing, arguing, reading. They are out of earshot, and frankly I don't mind. Outside, my husband is building a chicken coop for our new yard birds, and I am downright giddy about it. Even though we live in the city, our neighborhood is hen-friendly and we are not the first to host a small flock on our block. I have been begging for chickens for over a year, tearing out magazine articles about how to care for them, about which breeds are best for laying, for city life, and so forth. I have even gone so far as to visit a writer's blog where you can watch her yard birds via web cam. You might say I have been a tad obsessed.

89

Finally, in an act of compassion for me and prodding for Nathan, our friends and fellow chicken-owners Jeanetta and Ben brought us four fluffy baby chicks. This meant a coop had to be built. No more mulling. No more stalling.

Nathan is pretty handy, but a carpenter's son he is not. An electrician's son, yes. A pastor's kid, a nurse's kid, yes. But a master carpenter's? No. He is skilled enough to tackle this sort of project but, by his own admission, he is not skilled enough for it to be a fast process. Taking this truth into consideration, he has gone to great lengths to be prepared. He has sketched out his design several times. He has measured and measured and measured some more. For weeks he has turned this project over in his mind, thinking and figuring. Never the one to take the easy (and often more expensive) route, he is assembling our coop from an assortment of found parts. The walls are to be made from vintage doors and windows I have scavenged off the side of the road over time. Fresh-cut wood, purchased at the big-box hardware store down the street, is the frame; sheets of metal are the roof. Since the project has begun, this man of mine has built, torn down, rebuilt, and built again. We are on day ten, and he has gotten only as far as three framed walls, but I cannot fault him. Building a sturdy structure that can support living creatures is no small task. I don't know that I would have the patience for carpentry. The real kind.

I sit in my kitchen and tap at my keyboard, making mistakes, quickly hitting the delete and backspace buttons, cutting and pasting at will. All mistakes are corrected in the blink of an eye. My toes are cold so I tuck them under me while I continue to type. I say a little prayer of thanks that our new ductwork was well worth the hefty price tag, and I also say a prayer of thanks that my ever generous in-laws were able to help us make it happen. Outside, in the humidity of an early Arkansas spring heat wave, my husband Nathan swings his hammer time and time again, nailing piece after piece together, only to rip it all apart when he realizes he has made a miscalculation, one small error that makes the whole thing perilous. Sweaty and tired, he must undo the past couple of hours of work and begin again. He needs to get it right. He wants it to be done well. He needs it to last. These things matter, even for a little backyard chicken coop.

I close the computer and wander out to the back porch. Across the yard, Nathan is still at it. I see him pull down a section of wall he had just finished; it has missed perfection by inches. Through all of this doing and undoing his frustration never explodes, never overflows. I think about why that is. Is it because he is a saint? Never prone to anger? No. I live with the man. He is plenty human, especially where his temper is concerned. Is it because he just doesn't care if he has to redo every step five times? Is he that laidback? Again, no, that is not the reason—trust me. I finally settle on the idea that it must have something to do with expectations. When it comes to his carpentry skills, my husband is very aware of his limitations. He didn't expect to get it right the first time. He knew himself, and he knew his deficits. He faced them honestly. Had he expected to build the coop with the skill of a licensed contractor, quickly and with few hiccups, the outcome might have been different, his frustration wider, deeper, louder.

My life is like building that chicken coop. I make plans, and all too often I have to tear them up and start again. Occasionally, I am wise and I remember that I am not supposed to know the answers the first time, or sometimes ever. I just have to try. Go slow. Measure twice and cut once. Maybe measure four times. Maybe cut three times. Risk, trust, live. All too often I have to remind myself that what I tell my children is true also for me; that there is no shame in the starting over, in the tearing down and rebuilding. Tearing down and rebuilding is how God likes to work best. Isn't that what Creation is—birth to death to birth again, and on and on?

I think of Joseph, all those dreams and visits from angels, each time the messenger giving Joseph only the next step, not the full blueprint of God's plan. I imagine him waking after each dream, groggy, shaking his head, saying, "Again? You want us to go where? To do what? Are you going to tell me why?" From where I sit on my porch swing, I can see that Joseph was part of the bigger picture, an epic love story. But it probably didn't feel epic to him. It probably felt a lot like building a chicken coop out of scraps, full of the most ordinary and exhausting details, like packing and unpacking after each unexpected journey, lots of "try, try, try again" moments. Perhaps this is why Jesus was thirty before he started his ministry as we know it. Perhaps he had learned at the feet of Joseph, an everyday carpenter, what it would take to be fully ready to build something so bold, so absurd, so necessary, and so unorthodox as his church.

Children's St. Joseph's Day Party

Learning can be fun, even about members of our faith family who are long gone. Why not turn a little history lesson about Joseph's role in God's Story and his example of obedience into a fun evening of games, crafts, and a yummy dinner?

Wylie's Sawdust Lasagna Recipe

In Italy, the Feast of St. Joseph is often celebrated with what we call in the American South "Sunday potluck." One dish that is often served is a meatless pasta dish with a breadcrumb topping to represent the sawdust of a carpenter. I thought that lasagna, a dish that has to be built carefully, layer by layer like a house, would be the perfect dish for a St. Joseph's Day party. Since lasagna is Wylie's favorite food, he and Nathan developed this recipe together.

Ingredients

1   pound bacon cut into bite-size pieces, cooked crisp and drained

1   pound ground beef chuck, browned and drained

1   pound ground pork, browned and drained

1   cup grated Parmesan cheese

3   cups shredded mozzarella cheese

1   15-ounce tub ricotta cheese

1   24-ounce jar of your favorite prepared marinara sauce

1   15-ounce jar of your favorite prepared Alfredo sauce

1   6–7-ounce jar of prepared pesto sauce

1   egg
    Prepared Italian or Panko bread crumbs

2   boxes lasagna noodles (We prefer the smaller square pasta sheets that have no ruffled edges and do not need to be pre-boiled. You probably will not use all of both boxes, but you will likely need more than one.)

Directions

Preheat the oven to 400 degrees.

The best way to build a pan of lasagna is to first create a buffet of the various ingredients.

Mix the cooked meats together in a large bowl.

Mix the Parmesan and mozzarella in another large bowl.

Put the ricotta in a third bowl and mix in the egg.

Pour the marinara sauce into a fourth bowl (fairly good-sized) and then refill your sauce jar with tap water, and mix this into your marinara sauce. (The extra water will be absorbed by the lasagna noodles, which will enter the baking pan *uncooked.*)

In a large lasagna pan, spread a layer of the thin red sauce, completely covering the bottom of your pan.

Next place a layer of uncooked pasta on top of the sauce, followed by layers of Alfredo sauce, meat, mozzarella/Parmesan, pesto, and ricotta/egg.

Continue building layers in this fashion until you reach the top of the pan, always starting with the thin sauce.

The top layer should be composed in this way: marinara sauce, pasta, marinara sauce, mozzarella/Parmesan.

Cover dish tightly with foil and place on the center rack of the oven for about 30 minutes, or until it has thoroughly cooked through.

Remove foil, sprinkle with bread crumbs, and return to oven until cheese and bread crumbs are browned.

Let stand for 15 minutes before cutting into portions (if you do not let it stand and cool, the whole dish will fall apart into a slippery mess when you try to cut it.)

Embellishing Carpenter Aprons

I love it when something is as useful as it is cute. These carpenter aprons are a great party favor for every kid because they are useful both at the party and afterward. If you have a particularly crafty bunch of kids at your St. Joseph's party, it may be a good idea to incorporate the decorating of the aprons into the party schedule. However, if you think that it might be a bit too much to tackle, you can embellish them all before the party and hand them out as party favors.

Materials Needed

- 1 carpenter apron per party guest (You can purchase these aprons online or in local hardware stores.)
- Fabric markers or paints
- Flat-backed buttons
- Hot glue
- Fabric glue
- Fabric pre-washed and cut out into various shapes (I chose triangles, but circles and dots would be cute too.)
- Package of iron-on fusible interfacing
- Damp all-cotton towel
- Spray water bottle
- Scissors
- Iron, ironing board
- Other embellishments (beads, sequins, ribbon, fabric tape)

Directions

Pre-wash the aprons before your party. This will make them softer and easier to work with.

On a well-protected table, lay out the items that the kids can use by themselves—markers, paint, fabric glue, fabrics, embellishments, and so on.

Allow each kid to pick her or his apron and find a place at the table to use as an art station. There they can embellish their aprons using the fabric-friendly markers, crayons, and paints.

At a separate station close by (perhaps a card table or buffet table), set up your hot glue gun and ironing station.

If the kids want to attach fabric pieces to their aprons, you will need to cut an identical shape to the one (or ones) that kids want to use from the fusible interfacing. Following the directions on the interfacing package, adhere the fabric to the apron with the iron, then let cool.

To attached buttons or sequins, have a mending kit on hand. Have older children help the younger children attach these items.

Old Joseph Playing Cards

These cards are easy to make and great to give—as a gift, wrapped up in a carpenter apron, as a party favor, or just as a rainy-day surprise. You can use them to play a game of Memory with smaller kids, Old Joseph (play it as you would Old Maid, making sure to leave one of the Old Joseph cards out when you deal your deck), or for the truly advanced, see if you can build a house of cards, practicing patience, balance, and dedication.

Materials Needed

- Cardstock-weight scrapbook paper or thin-weight scrapbook paper and solid cardstock
- White printer paper or cardstock
- Color printer or copier
- Glue stick
- Scissors

Directions

Make two copies of each of the playing card images found in chapter 23, with the exception of the instructions and title card.

Print these on white cardstock or copy paper.

Cut each card image out, leaving a thin white border around all four edges.

Next cut your card bases out, using the template provided. You can round your edges (as I did) or leave them sharp.

Cut 29 Side-A bases using all the same patterned paper.

Cut 29 Side-B bases using as many patterns as you want.

Creating pairs, glue 1 Side-A base to 1 Side-B base.

Repeat until all have been glued. This creates your final playing card base.

Pick 3 cards and set aside.

Next, glue 1 card image (tools and Old Joseph) to Side B of the remaining 26 pairs, then set them aside.

Glue the 3 remaining images (Title Card, How-To Card, and About Card) to the 3 base pairs you set aside earlier. Remember to glue the images to the B side of each of the 3 cards.

If you are giving the cards as a gift, you can tie them up with twine and use a screw, bolt, and washer instead of a bow to embellish.

chapter 11

Palm Sunday

The Sunday Before Easter

Years went by and I accepted that I cannot
know the unknowable; that I must bring my beliefs
into the kitchen, make them work in this world. Finally
I realized that though I was not God, I was *of* God.

—**Nevada Barr,** *Seeking Enlightenment . . . Hat by Hat*

I have a word that sums me up. A word that perfectly describes so many things about my life. It is the word *found. I am found. I find. I have been found. I am finding.* These are phrases that seem to fit so many of the key moments and incidents of my life. I have been found by Christ's love and mercy. I am finding that the older I get, the less I know. I find the best treasures in the most unlikely of places.

There are people in this world who can set out to do something and then just do it, whatever "it" may be. They prosper under the weight of ambition. They can create mission statements, set goals, diligently map out their route using spreadsheets and bar graphs, and miraculously somehow it works. Their lives chug along like a well-organized military maneuvers; things are precise, expectations are met or exceeded, contingency plans are always in place, although rarely needed. I however am not that

97

person, I never have been, and I suspect that I never will be. The truth of my life is that I trip over things, often tumbling headfirst into them, stubbing my toes and bumping my head on the way down. All the best things in my life have been found this way: husband, friends, children, homes, churches, kitchen chairs, jobs. I have stumbled across them on my way to something else, something I thought was better.

Even though this trend can feel magical and adventurous, it mostly feels like a second-hand, second-choice way to live, as if my whole life were composed of things found on the curb or in dusty thrift stores, always someone else's rejects and castoffs. At times I wonder if there will ever come the day when I will walk into a store, any store, with a fist full of cash, clear blueprint in hand, and buy everything I need and want in a one-stop shopping extravaganza. But even in the daydream, I hear the whisper, *Is that what you want your life to look like?* murmuring from inside my heart. *No*, I answer myself, because in truth I love my beautiful, messy, found life. This life of mine, decoupaged from all the bits and pieces that I find and that find me, is a wonderful, light-filled life unlike any other. It is like my most favorite treasures, found at a flea market on the bottom shelf, cracked and pasted back together.

Even the most daily of days is made up of these found moments, moments when I realize that I already have everything I have been searching for. Moments full of my children's laughter as they jump off the couch and onto a pile of pillows gathered from every room in the house, leaving a trail of blankets, unmade beds, and knocked-over chairs in their wake. It is found in the smiles and stories and voices rising in song together at our little ragtag community church, every single person there a unique, beautiful, found story. It is found in the kisses from a man who waited patiently for me to come around to the idea that we were meant to be together. It is found despite all my attempts to miss it in my search for something else, something better, grander.

Today was one of those murky days spent in search of something, anything other than what was. Plagued with frustration and exhaustion, heavy with emotion and insecurities, all the result of what Anne Lamott refers to as "bad mind" in *Traveling Mercies* and what Holly Golightly called "the Mean Reds" in *Breakfast at Tiffany's*. In other words, nothing was really wrong, and yet everything was all wrong. At church this morning, sitting in the back, tears welling up at the strangest of times, my mind whirling and fuzzy, I was completely overwhelmed by everything on my plate—a book deadline looming, a full-time job at the peak of busyness, two kids' birthday parties to plan, my pastoral duties at church, not to mention the laundry piling up, the bills coming due, and a pedicure I desperately wanted but had no budget for. This compounded the guilt I felt. I should be grateful for the laundry—at least I have clothes to wash and somewhere to wash them. At least I have a job and one I like. How could I be so ungrateful?

I snuck out the back door during the last song, wanting to avoid the loving kindness of my church family, which would surely lead to more tears on my part and would require explanations I wasn't sure I could give. Who wants to comfort someone who is crying over the amount of laundry piling up? The contradiction, of course, is that I would have counseled anyone else to stay, to accept the love and prayers and hugs. But in my brokenness, my fear, my pride, and my self-justification that no one needs to be bothered with my laundry drama, I ran. I abandoned the opportunity to accept their love and my own advice, causing me further self-condemnation as my eyes again filled with tears and I backed my car out of the parking lot.

When I pulled around the back of the church building, I noticed an old metal lawn chair sticking out of the dumpster. I wasn't looking for an old metal chair, but there it was, in the dumpster. I slammed on my brakes, put the car in park, and hopped out. *Maybe it is just a* piece *of a chair*, I thought as I peered in, not daring to hope that anyone would throw such a treasure away. I saw not one but two vintage metal lawn chairs, robin's egg blue, perfectly faded and rusted. Suddenly, for a moment, all murkiness and tears were gone. I reached into the dumpster and pulled those chairs out, stuffing them—grime and all—in the back of my car. They were old and crusty and imperfect. They were in need of rescuing, in need of a home. I could not help but smile, and my heart leaped with gratitude and joy as I snatched them up. They may look like rusty, old, useless things to some, but to me they were little sticky love notes, placed exactly where I would see them, when I needed them most. I wish I could say that those chairs were enough to make me park my car and go back inside, but I still refused. I was too filled with my desire to keep going, my determination to flee, my dedication to stick to my plan.

Back at home I unloaded the chairs and looked at them sitting in the backyard with all the others that I have found over the years. The mesh ones, the bucket ones, the wooden Adirondack—all found in the trash. Each chair its own found story. I imagined them all filled with friends and family for a spring evening gathering, a birthday party, Easter, and a wave of regret and repentance flowed over me. I prayed for forgiveness for running when I should have stayed. For wanting to hide my ugliness, my chipped and rusty heart, instead of bringing it into the light, and laying it bare in the circle of community. How could I forget that rusty and crusty is how I have been found and is the hope for us all? That rusty and crusty, found in the trash dump, is God's favorite place to go shopping? He has never had it any other way. Even his most grand entrance was imperfect and impromptu—a moment filled with found objects and found memories. A moment where the simple and the second-hand—a borrowed donkey, dusty cloaks, broken tree branches, a carpenter-king, a common community—are the humble beginnings of what is now our Holy Week.

Found Hostess Apron
with Palm Leaves

This is the sort of sewing project that is great for beginners because it allows a lot of room for "creative interpretation," and there are enough elements that both young and old crafters can participate on some level. The idea is to use what you have on hand as best you can, following the example of those who celebrated on that first Palm Sunday with what they found within arms' reach. Imperfect, authentic, and easy, using those "palms" we have been given, unique to us, and always available to serve others and celebrate together.

Materials Needed

- Hand towel (1 for each apron)
  (I purchased all the ones used for this
  project from a thrift store.)
- Various fabrics in complementary colors
  —a total of 1½ yards
- Pocket fabric, cut 12 x 5 inches
- Sewing machine
- Thread
- Pencil
- Plain paper
- Printer

Directions

Find some hands, little and big, to trace. Trace 1 left hand and 1 right hand onto a plain piece of paper. You will need roughly 5 hands per apron.

Next, cut out the hands. These will be your patterns. You can now use your hand patterns to trace.

Next you create a "branch stem" pattern using the pattern in chapter 23. Enlarge this pattern, then cut it out and use it to create your palm frond branch stem.

Iron all your pieces of fabric, including your towel.

Lay your towel face up, lengthwise, and set aside.

Fold pocket fabric in half lengthwise and press so that it now measures 5 x 6 inches.

Next, place pocket at a comfortable height on the left side of your towel. (I placed mine 4 inches in from the left edge and 3½ inches down from the top edge of my towel.)

Make sure the folded edge is facing the top of your towel.

Press, pin, and topstitch ¼-inch from the raw edges along the 3 sides, leaving the top of the pocket open.

Pin your palm stem at a diagonal, to the right of your pocket. The end of your stem should rest toward the bottom center edge of your apron and lean toward the right.

Working from the top down, pin your palms.

Place the largest palm at the top of your stem.

Arrange your remaining palms in a fan shape, moving down the stem, largest to smallest.

Your smallest palm should be the bottom and overlap the tip of your stem.

For extra security you can use a glue stick and glue your palms and stem down to help keep them in place while you pin, press, and stitch.

Once all of your palms are pinned, press.

Topstitch palm frond to the towel beginning at the bottom of the stem, and running your stitch through the center of each finger.

You can use a straight topstitch for this or a zigzag stitch for added texture.

Repeat, running your second stitch line slightly to the right or left of your original stitch.

Note: there is no perfect way of doing this. The goal is to secure your stem and each finger, while still allowing the raw edges some movement.

Once your palms are secure, press and set aside.

To create the waistband and ties, you will need to cut two long strips of fabric 6 inches wide across the width of your fabric.

Stitch together these strips, end to end, creating one long strip.

Fold this strip in half lengthwise, and then again.

The length of fabric should now be 1½ inches wide and folded into 4 layers.

Press.

Find the center of your waistband. (This will be where you stitched your 2 ends together.) I like to find the center by folding my towel in half and pressing to create a center crease.

Lay your waistband down lengthwise with the fold at the top and the opening at the bottom.

Open waistband at the center fold.

Line up the center of your waistband with the center of your towel, and place top edge of towel between folds of waistband, encasing the top edge of your towel between all four layers.

Zigzag or straight-stitch a topstitch ¼ inch from raw edge.

Press again.

The final step is to wash your apron. Each apron will look a little different, and the rough cut-out fabric hands will fray a bit in the wash, helping to complete the palm frond look.

chapter 12

Maundy Thursday

The Thursday Before Easter

Some things don't matter much. Like the color of a house.
How big is that in the overall scheme of life? But lifting a
person's heart—now, that matters. The whole problem with
people is . . . they know what matters, but they don't choose
it. . . . The hardest thing on earth is choosing what matters.
Sue Monk Kidd, *The Secret Life of Bees*

Looking back, it occurs to me now that God uses food and the domestic rituals that surround it to call me into his presence. It is his love language to me. Leftover roast beef sandwiches, bowls of ice cream topped with Grape-Nuts cereal, and sixty-nine-cent boxes of macaroni and cheese are just a few of the meals that have brought peace, love, hope, and healing into my life because of whom I shared them with.

Out of my father's family of four brothers, he was the only one to ever move away from Little Rock, and not just out of town but out of state. Because of this scandalous action, coming back to my parents' hometown was always a grand event; the eldest son coming home with his family never went unnoticed. My parents, making do on a pastor's salary with a family of six, could not afford grand family vacations, so we simply returned to Arkansas to visit family instead, free lodging and meals being part of the appeal.

My father's family is large, and as a child I saw it not only as "large" but also as "larger than life." Granddaddy, my paternal grandfather, was a well-known and respected Southern Baptist pastor, and my uncles ranged from traveling evangelist to track star to the local version of Ferris Bueller. Nana, my father's mother, was an amazing cook, preparing a best-of-southern-cooking spread each time she stepped into the kitchen. Often our trips home to Little Rock coincided with major events including holidays, ordination services, revival weeks, and weddings, all of which birthed my favorite part of coming home, Sunday evening gatherings at Nana and Granddaddy's.

In those days, before everyone grew up and grew apart, my grandparents' house was a wonderful gathering place for friends and family, especially after church services. Their ranch-style home has the perfect hallway for pint-sized football games and wrestling sessions, its main attribute being its length. On those nights the formal living and dining rooms were filled with people lingering and talking over plates piled high with fried chicken, black-eyed peas, mashed potatoes, sautéed squash, sweet corn on the cob, chicken-n-dumplings, cornbread and rolls, pies, and pound cakes. In the background, grown-ups and kids tinkered on the piano, often a full-on gospel quartet forming, or the guest of honor would take the hot seat, leading everyone in a round of rousing hymns, Nana's and Aunt Zada's alto vibratos rising above the baritones and tenors of my father and uncles.

In the family room, football was most likely on the TV, children darting in and out, playing hide-and-seek and grabbing bites of rolls and honey-baked ham in between their games. I can remember my Aunt Kathy sitting on her husband's lap and my thinking how scandalous it was for grown-ups to behave that way in public. Looking back, I realize they were all of twenty-two years of age.

My family is broken like most everyone's. We have our skeletons, our fights, our heartbreaks, our wounded pride and feelings. As I have grown up, the bloom has come off the family rose quite a bit, but what I have come to is this: regardless of what my experiences of family have been as an adult, I will not let it diminish the love and warmth I felt as a child in those moments—the feeling that I was the luckiest girl in the world to be a part of something so magical: all the laughter, all the singing, all the great food, the intense discussions, the storytelling. These nights were a powerful life force that enveloped me, comforted me, and inspired me. These nights were also my first impressions of what great dinner parties should be like.

In 2006, Nathan and I were at the very end of our time at a church we loved dearly, where we had been married, had our babies dedicated, and met some of our very best friends. We had both served in leadership. I had served on the staff, and one of my uncles was the pastor. There were a lot of reasons for leaving. Good ones, bad ones, almost all heartbreaking and every last one a part of growing up, of making my own way in the world. Even though I could feel the tidal wave of change coming, I could not leave without one last attempt to find my footing, to hold on to what had been, what I hoped could be, and what I believed down in my gut was still possible. The little girl in me still longed for what I had found all those years ago at my grandparents' home: evenings of love and laughter, deep discussions and tall tales, all shared over a table covered in homemade deliciousness.

So I proposed we start a series of "Dinner for Eight" groups in the church. Eight people would get together once a month for six months and have dinner and, in theory, we would pour all the names back into the pot and start over. The idea was that this would help people who had never connected before to find connections, friendships, community. Because we wanted the first round to be especially successful, a lot of thought went into pairing up the groups. Groups were assigned based on what members had checked on their interest form. For instance, what night was best, if they wanted a kid-friendly group, or if they wanted to eat at homes or in restaurants. We also wanted to make sure everyone had at least one other person they knew in their group in order to provide a feeling of safety right away. I have to confess that somewhere in the back of my mind was the hope that I could stack the deck of my particular Dinner for Eight group: to pick those people that I had always wanted to be friends with but never had the chance. Now, only half joking, I say that Dinner for Eight was my parting gift to myself.

Deep down, I knew that our season in that community was about to end, and to soften the blow I created this little group as my cushion. I chose the members of my group for their wisdom (two of the couples were older than we were, one even old enough to be our parents), for their experience in just the sort of thing we were about to weather, for their authenticity, for the fact that their children enjoyed them and wanted to be with them even as adults. These were all qualities that drew me to them because I knew that Nathan and I were going to need a lot of wisdom and prayer during this next season.

That autumn we began to meet and to talk and drink lots of wine and eat lots and lots of amazing food. (I may have also taken into account their cooking ability for my selections.) Eventually, as life has a pattern of doing, the group changed a bit, members were added, members moved on. In the past five years of dining together, our little group has experienced divorce, marriage, illness, sick kids, estranged family members, cancer, vacations, holiday gatherings. There have been surprise pregnancies and surprise grandchildren and surprise career changes. And through all of those things there have been abundant blessings and tears, but mostly, dearly, there has been healing. What was once "Dinner for Eight" has grown to "Dinner for Twelve" with sometimes a few more or a few less depending on who is in town.

Now when we gather and I look around the table, I am not just looking at the faces of my friends but at the faces of my family. After all, these are the ones with whom we have shared every hope, fear, obstacle, dream, and frustration over the past five years. They have prayed with us and for us. I am humbled, and I cannot help but wonder if we have returned this love as well. I hope so. All our lives have changed in those five years, and yet here we still are, together, breaking bread, drinking wine, eating until we can't feel our toes, bursts of laughter peppering our conversations. In those moments I am home. I am a part of something magical yet again. Here there is great affection, and it heals me, filling in those places in my heart that feel hollowed out and lonely.

It is Maundy Thursday and we are all gathering to remember and honor Christ's last meal before his crucifixion. In my mind's eye I see the painting by Da Vinci, Christ in the middle, everyone to his left and his right with all the symbolism and conjecture that painting has brought. But did that meal convene in the picture-perfect, ready-for-their-close-up gathering so artfully portrayed? Chances are they were all bunched around one table, heads close together, looking into each other's eyes and hearts, passing the broken bread and wine back and forth across the table, bumping elbows, sharing stories of Passover meals before, complimenting the cook on the texture of the bread or the richness of the meal.

Christ knew that this was his last night to walk with his brothers in community, and this is how he chose to spend it—with his friends, first over dinner and then in prayer. He could have done everything differently. He could have gone to the races and bet his last buck. Jesus could have closed himself away in a fancy hotel room and eaten the richest of foods and drunk the best wine money could buy, all alone. He could have chosen so many more decadent things. So many more private things. So many more safe things. But he did not. He honored the traditions of his faith by observing the Passover supper, and he chose to do it with the friends with whom he had shared everything: the good, the bad, and the wonderful. The sickness and the healing and the questions and the frustrations. They had seen it all, been through it all with him. They were his chosen family, and this is how he spent his last hours of freedom. This is the example he gave us to follow.

Seder Supper Southern-Style

The Seder Supper, the traditional Passover supper, is a meal I was lucky enough to experience growing up in our little Baptist church in Juneau, Alaska, where my father was the pastor. For our family, I have developed a modified version of the Seder dinner, trying to keep the spirit and flavor the same, but with a southern-inspired twist. Also, while I love the symbolism of the Seder Supper, Maundy Thursday is a school night around our house, and although we try to gather with our friends to remember this night, it is essential to everyone's sanity that the meal is practical, enjoyable, and edible for all ages.

MAUNDY THURSDAY

Ms. J's Chicken and Dumplings

This recipe is my answer to the matzo ball soup and the baked or roasted chicken that are a staple of the Seder Supper. Not being Jewish, but being southern, chicken and dumplings seemed like the perfect alternative to these traditional Seder dishes. And as for the recipe title, well, that comes from Sweet Man's nickname for me, in the southern tradition of Miss Ellie from the TV show *Dallas*.

This is a large recipe—enough for twelve adults. Note: You can use homemade or store-bought chicken stock, or a combination of both.

For the Broth

Bring 15 cups of chicken stock to a boil.

Add the following to the boiling liquid:

3 carrots, peeled, washed, and diced (optional)

3 celery stalks, washed and thinly sliced

1 medium yellow onion, diced

1 tablespoon of salt

4 pounds of boneless chicken breast (frozen or thawed)

Once the chicken breasts are fully cooked, pull them out, and set them aside to cool.

Reduce broth to simmer and leave simmering while you make the dumplings.

For the Dumplings

Mix together the following ingredients:

6 cups of flour

3 tablespoons of baking powder

3 teaspoons of salt

Next, cut in 1 cup of solid vegetable shortening (use either a pastry cutter or 2 table knives).

Once the shortening has been cut in well, begin adding ice cold water, ½ cup at a time, into the mixture. I use about 2¼ cup of ice water (sometimes I use more, sometimes I use less, depending on the humidity in the air).

Your goal is to create a dough that is soft, smooth, and easy to roll out but is not leathery or mushy or grainy. Next, roll your dough out. These dumplings are southern-style flat dumplings like we make in Arkansas, not the round fluffy "drop" dumplings that are common in the North.

My good friend and baking mentor Lynn taught me this great kitchen **Tip**:

- When rolling out dough, spread out a smooth kitchen towel on your counter (I prefer the flour sack variety) and cover it with a good dusting of flour. This will be your rolling surface, and after you are done, you can simply fold the towel up and take it outside to shake off the excess.

Roll out the dough, using a slightly floured rolling pin, to between 1/8 and 1/4-inch thickness. Next, using a knife or pizza cutter, cut the dough into strips about 1 inch wide by 3 inches long.

Bring your stock back to a rolling boil, and tear the cooked chicken breast into bite-size pieces, adding it back to the liquid. Once that is done, begin adding the strips of dumpling dough into the stock. Once all the strips have been added, give the pot a good stir, and cover. Reduce the heat to a simmer. Check every few minutes, stirring gently, until the dumplings are tender and cooked through, about 15–20 minutes.

111

Nathan's Greens with Bacon

This portion of the dinner is to represent the bitter herbs and the salt water of a Seder Supper. Growing up I hated greens—collard, mustard, turnip. To me they smelled awful and tasted worse. But Nathan changed all of that for me by changing how he prepares them. Here is his answer to greens, southern-style.

Ingredients

4 bundles of mustard greens

1 large red onion, halved top to bottom, then cut into slices top to bottom

12-ounce package of cured salt pork, cut into matchsticks (I know it may be a bit odd to use pork in a meal that is in part meant to pay homage to a Jewish tradition, but frankly pork is an essential ingredient for good southern greens, and there is no other way around it. Eating Sweet Man's greens is one of those times I am especially glad to be a Gentile!)

2 cloves of garlic, minced

2 tablespoons of apple cider vinegar

Salt and pepper to taste

Directions

Clean the greens—this step is essential.

Remove stems from greens and discard. Wash leaves thoroughly in several changes of water until there is no more grit in the bottom of the sink after washing. Dry very thoroughly in a salad spinner or by pressing the greens between towels.

To cut the greens you will use a French technique called cutting a chiffonade.

Begin by stacking the leaves into piles, roll them into a tube like a cigar, and slice thinly crosswise down the length of the tube. This will make thin ribbons of greens.

Place a large skillet over medium-high heat and cook the salt pork until it has rendered most of its fat and has become crisp.

Pour off all of the grease from the pan except for about 2 tablespoons.

Add the onion and cook until tender.

Add the garlic and stir.

Add in the greens by handfuls while continually stirring. (The greens will be too large at this point to fit in the skillet all at once, but will quickly cook down and make room for another batch.)

Once all of the greens have made it into the pan, add the vinegar. Continue to stir until all of the liquid exuded by the greens has evaporated. Taste for salt and pepper. You will likely not need to add any salt, as there is a great deal in the cured pork.

chapter 13

Holy Saturday

The Day Before Easter

I do not believe that sheer suffering teaches. If suffering alone taught, all the world would be wise, since everyone suffers. To suffering must be added mourning, understanding, patience, love, openness, and the willingness to remain vulnerable.
—**Anne Morrow Lindbergh,** *Hour of Gold, Hour of Lead*

There is no other place in the world I would rather be than at my Maw and Paw's house. Their home has always been my refuge, my happy place. The pace there is slow and tranquil. In typical grandparent fashion, their house is technology-lite: dial-up Internet, limited cable, questionable cell coverage.

I don't go to their house to get things done. I go there to stop. To sit. To listen. To wait. I go there when the questions have gotten so loud inside my head that I cannot hear anything else. I go when I need to cry tears that I cannot explain. I go and I sit at the kitchen table, where in the summer we eat fresh Arkansas tomatoes with every meal. I sit on their porch, gently sway in the swing, stare at nothing but the sun on the trees. And then, when I least expect it, peace seeps in and restores me.

113

HOLY SATURDAY

This home, this porch, this kitchen, this is where I spend Holy Saturday. Thanks to my Southern Baptist upbringing, I was already married and a mother before I realized that the Saturday before Easter even had an official name. Holy Saturday. The name sounds so formal. So lily-white. In reality, it is anything but.

My mother's family all gathers at Maw and Paw's house the weekend of Easter. Some roll in on Friday night, some on Saturday. We gather in the kitchen, cramming as many bodies as we can around a four-person table, to drink endless cups of coffee, share magazines, and solve the world's problems. We are there to celebrate the resurrection of Christ. We are also there to feast on the favorite family meal: Granny Mary's kitchen sink soup and Presbyterian slaw. The soup comes from my great-grandmother's kitchen in Mississippi. The slaw, according to family legend, comes from a church potluck, after which my grandfather insisted my grandmother track down a recipe for that crunchy, tangy "Presbyterian slaw."

The only drawback to this meal is that we have to wait all day before we can chow down. So while the soup is stewing and the slaw is soaking, we do the only logical thing to do on Holy Saturday: we all dye eggs. Dozens and dozens of eggs. Not long after my sister Jemimah married Adam, someone made the discovery that my new brother-in-law had never *in his entire life* dyed an Easter egg. I think we probably all looked at him as if he had just announced that he was from the planet Mars. Of course, being the overly enthusiastic crafty crew that we are, we immediately went to boiling eggs, setting out coffee mugs, filling them with water and vinegar and little pellets of dye, covering every inch of the kitchen table with newsprint, and demanding that he sit down and get to it. Dyeing eggs is an all-hands-on-deck, all-ages-welcome tradition in my family. Everyone tries his or her hand at dyeing a couple of eggs, and often there is a healthy bit of competition to see who can create the most unique, out-of-the-carton egg. Different techniques are employed—the tie-dye, the rubber-band-wrapped, the half-n-half, the marbled, the blown—and everyone fights over the tools.

The one technique out of all that we have tried that requires the most trust, despite its simplicity, is the wax crayon. With the wax-crayon technique, you must take the translucent waxy crayon that came in your egg-dye kit and draw a variety of shapes, designs, or letters on your egg—the catch being that you cannot see what you are drawing. You cannot see if your flower looks like a flower or your letter *J* like a *J*. The only evidence that you have done anything at all to your poor little egg are the bits of wax here and there that have clumped up on the egg's glossy white surface. After the wax comes the dye. You place your egg in a cup, pink or yellow or blue, and you wait. And wait. And wait some more. If you are at Maw's house, you will probably get up for another cup of coffee and go stare into the soup pot, trying to will the potatoes to cook faster. Eventually, enough time passes and you go back to the table and pull your egg out to see if, in fact, the flower is a flower, the letter *J* is the letter *J*.

To me, Holy Saturday is that wax-crayon day. It is the day that we wait. It is the day that Mary waited, that Peter and Simon and James waited. The day that Joseph of Arimathea waited. As I dye my eggs and prepare for Easter Sunday, as I finally get to sit down for my dinner of soup, slaw, and cornbread, I look around at all the people I love and I try to imagine life without them for even one day. My heart sinks at the thought. I know it is inevitable, but yet it seems so impossible. It is also inevitable that when the time comes, and we are separated, there will be no third-day resurrection. The answer will be final. Mortal death is ordinary that way.

But Holy Saturday is in fact holy because it was not ordinary. This was not an ordinary death; this was not an ordinary day. Christ, the Messiah, had been crucified. He was in the tomb, and no one knew how it would all turn out. Was it all

115

in vain? Had they not understood? Was he not who they believed him to be? Would he ever come back, or was it all over? Would he really rise in three days? Did they dare hope? The questions, the sadness, the loss, even the shreds of hope that must have come over them—I can only imagine it as overwhelming.

On Holy Saturday I do my best to live in that place, that wax-crayon place of trust and waiting. Of accepting what I cannot know. Of mourning what needs to be mourned. Of accepting what needs to be accepted. Of hoping for what seems impossible.

Sailboat Easter Baskets

I am always trying to create new crafts that my boys will enjoy making and playing with as well. I designed these boats with Easter in mind, but they have also played host to Lego and Star Wars characters on the occasional bathtub excursion. When we made these for Easter, we talked about all of Jesus's friends—the disciples who had been fishermen. Although the Scriptures give us some indication of what some of the disciples did on Good Friday and on Easter Sunday, not much is said about their actions on Saturday. I like to think that a few of them went fishing to sort things out. To sit, to pray, to hope, and to wait.

Materials Needed

- Red plaid paper food baskets (You can get these at most restaurant supply stores or online.)
- Modeling clay (2-inch square)
- Bamboo skewer
- 12 x 12-inch scrapbook paper
- Scrapbook paper scraps
- Tape
- Glue stick
- Scissors
- Easter grass

Directions

Place your square of clay into your food basket, off to the left side, toward the edge. Press down until the clay is stuck well enough to what is now the sailboat floor. The clay will not adhere permanently.

Using the pattern provided in chapter 23, cut out your sail. Fold a 12 x 12-inch sheet of paper in half and place the pattern on the fold. Cut triangle out.

Next, secure your sail to your bamboo skewer. Lay the skewer on the inside of your sail in the center crease, fixing it in place with a small piece of tape.

Using the glue stick, trace the inside edges of your sail. Once all edges have a thick layer of glue, close your sail around your skewer and press flat, smoothing out any wrinkles. This makes a double layer of sail for strength.

Embellish your sail with extra bits of paper, stickers, glitter, ribbon, or other ephemera. I use torn pieces of paper for a "patched" sail look on mine.

Finally, stick the skewer into the clay and voilà! You have a sailboat.

Fill with Easter grass, candies, and Easter eggs.

Presbyterian Slaw

This recipe is a family favorite. My grandmother makes it to go with her kitchen sink soup, and we always find ourselves eating it on Holy Saturday. The flavor is sweet and tangy, and the texture is crisp. It is best to make it first thing in the day or even the night before so it can "soak" properly.

Ingredients for Salad

In a large bowl combine:

1 head of cabbage, torn into pieces, about corn-chip size (do not shred)

4 stalks of celery, diced

1 small bunch of green onions, diced

1 green bell pepper, diced

Ingredients for Dressing

1 cup of white vinegar

1½ to 2 cups of sugar (depending on how sweet you like it)

1 cup of sunflower or canola oil

2 tablespoons of whole celery seed

2 teaspoons of salt

Black pepper to taste

Directions

In a small saucepan, mix dressing ingredients and bring to a quick boil. Reduce heat, stirring mixture until sugar is dissolved. Remove immediately from heat and allow the dressing to cool slightly.

Once the dressing is no longer boiling hot, pour over cabbage and vegetable mixture and place in refrigerator to soak until chilled. The longer the slaw soaks, the better it is.

Granny Mary's Kitchen Sink Soup

My grandmother began making this soup from my great-grandmother's recipe on days that everyone is expected at her house because, although our family is very talented at many things, punctuality is not one of them. "Well, soup will keep," she says, to anyone who calls to report their reason (excuse) for running late. And she is right. No matter what time we finally all gather around the table, the soup is hot and delicious.

Ingredients

- 1 pound of beef (Maw uses a small roast or stew meat, depending on what is on sale)
- 1 large can of tomatoes, whole or diced
- 2 large carrots, peeled and chopped
- 4 medium potatoes (any kind, although I like reds best), peeled and cubed
- 1 yellow onion, diced
- Salt to taste
- Black pepper to taste
- 2 teaspoons of chili powder
- 4 ounces of spaghetti
- ½ cup elbow macaroni
- ½ cup egg noodles
- Optional additional veggies:
- Red cabbage
- Green cabbage
- Celery
- Enough water to cover beef generously (perhaps 6–8 cups)

Directions

Place beef in a large stew pot with lots of water. Bring to a boil, then reduce heat to simmer. Leave for 1 hour. Next, add vegetables, including potatoes, and salt and pepper to taste. Cook on low for 30–40 minutes. You can then leave the pot on simmer for up to several hours. About 20 minutes before serving add the pasta. Once pasta is tender, the soup is ready to eat.

119

All my life I thought that the story was over when the hero and heroine were safely engaged—after all, what's good enough for Jane Austen ought to be good enough for anyone. But it's a lie. The story is about to begin, and every day will be a new piece of the plot.

—Mary Ann Shaffer and Annie Barrows, *The Guernsey Literary and Potato Peel Pie Society*

chapter 14

Easter

The Sunday Following Forty Days After Ash Wednesday

I was in second grade when I committed my first serious craft crime. The crime in question centers on my first solo sewing endeavor, and I am certain of the year because of the house we were living in. I can always date my memories by the houses in which they occurred (a beneficial by-product of moving often), and this memory takes place in the parsonage next door to my grandfather's church where we lived for six months between my father's seminary graduation and his securing a pastoral position. My family had left Memphis and returned to Little Rock to the familiar comfort of my grandparents, aunts, uncles, and cousins while my father looked for work. It was during that year that I grew interested in sewing crafts. Up until that time I had only ridden sidesaddle at the sewing machine pedal, sitting on my mother's lap, and at Maw's elbow, as they would stitch together a dress for me or a pair of shorts for my brother. I was allowed to help guide the fabric past the fast-moving needle as the thread tugged it here and there. If I was really lucky I got to press the pedal when they did a backstitch. By then I knew how to thread a needle, how to do a simple straight stitch by hand, and how to use a seam ripper, but I had not yet taken on a sewing project from start to finish by myself. That is, until the day of the Heart Project.

121

EASTER

I do not remember where the inspiration to make a small stuffed heart pillow came from, but I would bet a quarter that I saw something similar in one of my mother's magazines. What I do remember is that I was suddenly possessed by the urgent need to create something, and a pillow—shaped like a heart, with eyelet trim—is what I chose. Being a fairly obedient child, I asked my mother if I could use some of her fabric for a sewing project. She said yes and pointed me in the direction of her stash while she continued making dinner and tending to my younger siblings. Sitting on the floor of our den, I unfolded a beautiful piece of flannel fabric that was covered with tiny flowers in all the colors of the rainbow. Smoothing the fabric out, as I had seen my mother and grandmother do a hundred times, I attempted to pat down all the bumps and wrinkles I could, until I was sure everything was perfect. Then I folded the fabric in half lengthwise, remembering how to cut two shapes out at the same time, just as my mother had taught me. Next, using my marker, I drew a heart shape about ten inches in diameter dead center of the fabric, getting as close to the folded edge as I could. Using my mother's best fabric scissors, I cut both hearts out.

Pleased by my success thus far, I put the hearts face to face and began to pin the edges together—when in walked my mother. I proudly held up my heart, but instead of the smile I was expecting, all I saw was shock peppered with rage. My mother was not looking at me or my heart; she was looking at her fabric. Her favorite fabric. The fabric she had been saving for a special project, lying on the floor with a big double heart cut out of the middle, rendering it useless as one large piece of yardage.

I don't remember what she said. Did she yell? She wasn't typically a yeller. What was her tone? I know it was serious. My mother was not cruel in any way, but she always got her point across. And that day I learned my lessons well. I have never cut a hole in the middle of another yard of fabric since, and I always double-check before cutting someone else's fabric. Every single time. Now a mother with my own stash of fabric and rules, I look at my kids and wonder if they experience me this way as well. Will they remember my point years from now? Am I too harsh, too petulant, too calm, too rash, too reactionary? Do I yell more than I think I do? Am I not firm enough? I am not sure. It is hard to get outside of myself enough to know.

I eventually got to finish my heart pillow, and I know my mother did not discard that fabric, despite its ugly hole. I know this because it turned up in other projects later on and because my mother does not give up that easily; she will not be defeated by one mistake. Everything can be made new again. I also know this because it is what I do now when my children cut into my fabric in all the wrong places. When they use almost all of that one special ingredient I bought for that one special meal to conduct one of their many experiments instead. When they mix my paints together or cut up my favorite scrapbooking papers. When they dig up the flowerbed to bury their pirate treasure.

This is the beauty of Easter to me. Easter is the day when the broken and the wasted, the messed-up plans, the holes in the middle of favorite fabrics, the mistakes, the sins, and all the what-ifs are scooped up and remade in the beauty and mystery of the Resurrection. Christ did not arrive, live, die, or rule as anyone expected. Why would his Resurrection be anything other than the same? Easter can easily become one of those days in which I become more consumed with what my kids are wearing and what I am cooking than what we are celebrating: the Resurrection. Maybe this is because when I really get still and quiet enough to think hard about what I am saying I believe, then my hair starts to hurt a little and my shoes suddenly seem too tight. Resurrection. I believe in the Resurrection. I believe that a human man named Jesus is also God. That he died, descended into hell, and then rose again on the third day. Alive. When I am honest with myself I admit that I cannot really fathom what this means—and to say anything else would be to dishonor this day.

Paschal-Inspired Candle

The Paschal Candle is a candle that is lit either on Holy Saturday or on Easter. Its purpose is to represent Christ and the light his Resurrection brought to the world. Traditionally, the candle is lit and placed in a prominent place in the front of the church, where it remains lit from Easter until the end of the Easter season, on Ascension Sunday.

Although traditionally only one candle is needed to be the household Paschal Candle, you may have unhappy crafters if you limit the family to just one. If each child would like to make his or her own candle, I say go for it—they can either give them as gifts to families who perhaps would not have made their own Christ Candles, or you can allow them to each make their own candle and emphasize how it represents their own personal relationship with Christ.

Materials Needed

- 1 large white candle in glass jar
- Assortment of flat-backed buttons in a variety of colors and sizes
- Craft glue
- Fabric
- Paint brush
- Small bowl of water
- Hot glue gun and glue stick
- Large box of matches
- Coordinating scrapbook paper

Directions

The goal is to wrap your candle with your fabric and then add a cross design to the front.

To accomplish this, you will first need to measure out how much fabric you need. You can do this by placing your candle jar on the fabric and marking where you want to cut the top and the bottom of the fabric. Next wrap the piece of fabric around the circumference of the jar, marking again where you need to trim. Once you have figured the measurements, cut your fabric.

Next, with the paint brush, coat the outside of the jar (in all places where you want the fabric to adhere) with a thin coating of craft glue that has been mixed with just a bit of water.

Once the jar is thoroughly but thinly coated, wrap the fabric around the candle, working as you wrap to pull the fabric tight, smoothing out bubbles with your fingertips as you go.

To secure the fabric, run a bead of craft glue down the back edge, where the 2 ends overlap, then press closed and smooth.

Let dry.

To Create Your Cross

Start by picking a large focal-point button. This will serve as the anchor for your cross design.

Using hot glue adhere your large button to the fabric-covered jar.

Place your anchor button about 1 ½" down from the top of your jar.

Next, continue to add buttons using the hot glue, creating your cross design. I found that it was best to create the vertical line first and then the horizontal line.

If you would like to create a coordinating box of matches, you can cover an existing box, using scrapbook papers in coordinating colors and patterns. Simply use your matchbox as a template, tracing and then cutting out the right-size paper pieces.

Next attach them to the matchbox with a glue stick.

Last, glue 2 buttons to the top, using craft glue, to create a cohesive look.

Summer

joy

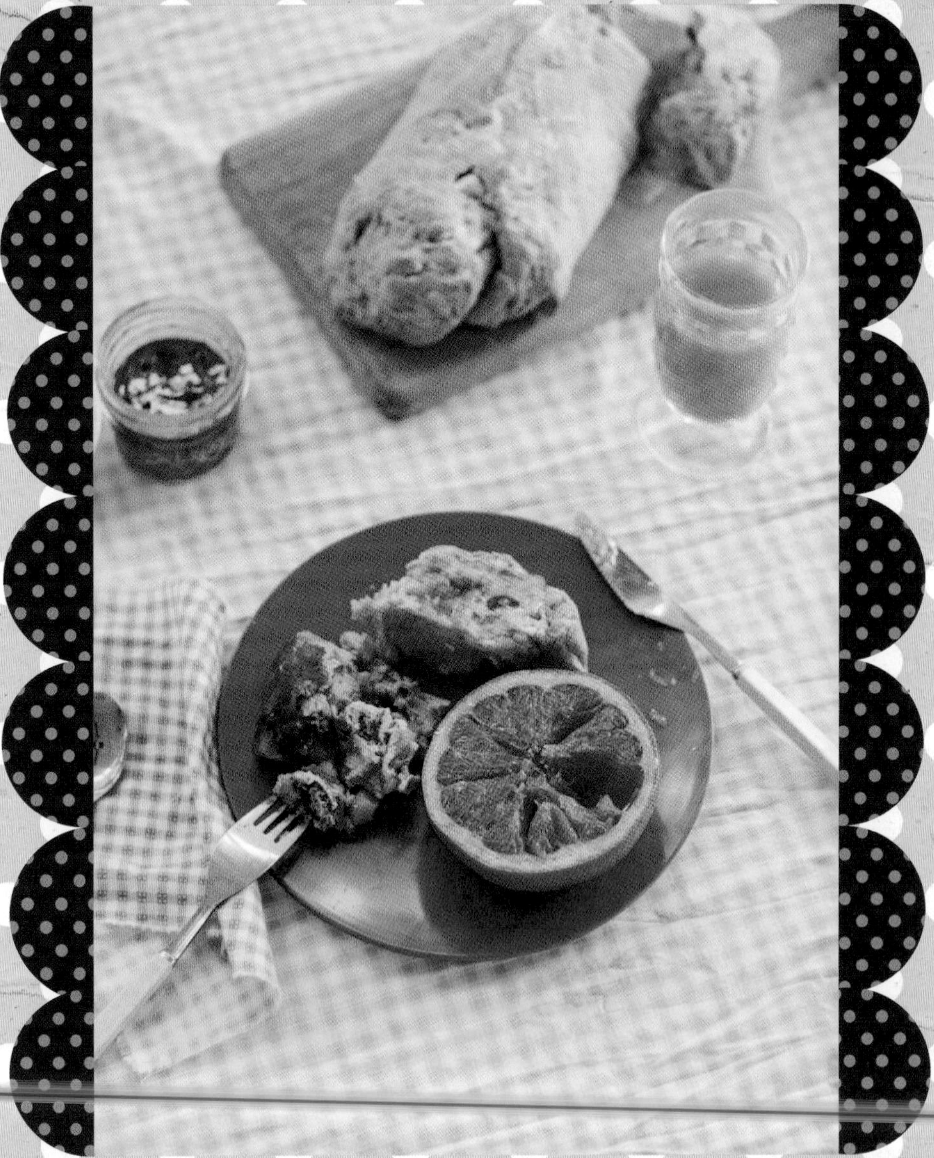

Pentecost Sunday

The Fiftieth Day After Easter

> Come not to speak, but to listen. Not to hear what is expected, But to be open to the ways the Spirit moves among you.
> —*Sing the Journey*

When Nathan and I got married we were very young and very broke. Luckily, our parents helped us out as much as they could with the wedding and honeymoon expenses. We went to New Orleans for our honeymoon—travel and lodging generously provided by my new in-laws, our pockets flush with all the twenty- and fifty-dollar bills that had been pressed into my new husband's hands during the reception.

We had chosen New Orleans for several reasons. We had both been there the previous spring but separately, at different times, and we were eager to experience the city together, to see it through each other's eyes. Another reason for our choice was that we had anticipated paying for the trip ourselves and therefore had limited our options to places we could drive to in a day. But despite all the other logical reasons, the greatest factor in our picking New Orleans was that I desperately wanted to go someplace that felt like a foreign country but where English was still the preferred language. In addition to our tight budget, I had this feeling that, being young and newly married, our honeymoon was not the best time to travel internationally. I was confident that as much as I loved my husband, our relationship was not ready to withstand the pressures of international travel. When you travel to a foreign land where you don't speak the language, you need to go with someone who makes it easy to navigate stressful situations. How I knew at age twenty-two that we were not quite that mature yet is beyond me. So on the day after our wedding, off we went.

The New Orleans we visited was the one that existed before Hurricane Katrina hit, before the World Trade Center towers collapsed, and before the housing market tanked. New Orleans in the spring of 1997 was bustling and vibrant, colorful and crowded, and we were in the middle of it all, bright-eyed and bushy-tailed. Finally, we were on our own, grown-up married adults (I use that term loosely in hindsight) left to navigate the wide berth of everything New Orleans and this thing called marriage had to offer. Most of the trip is a blur, as I suspect most good honeymoons are. I remember this and that, bits and pieces, but they are all vaguely translucent and fluid. I remember that it was hot, even for May. I remember that we walked everywhere, never venturing far outside the French Quarter out of fear that we would somehow be robbed of all our cash by savvy taxi drivers and overpriced tourist traps.

Our first night in the Big Easy, Nathan convinced me to go into some dive bar, where I watched a well-oiled and immoderately enthusiastic blues singer pull one girl after another out of the audience onto his stage to croon alongside him. Stiff with fright, sure he would pick me, I tried to look cool but not too cool. Scared but not too scared. I begged Nathan to promise that he would not let me be dragged onto that stage, no matter what, but he just laughed, and my fear increased. Somehow we made it through one round of drinks and back outside. And after that I picked the eating and drinking establishments.

Despite the slightly other-planet-ness of New Orleans, the slow-talking drawl, and the deep-fried, long-stewed, intoxicating smells, we were still on American soil. If I listened closely enough, I could understand the words coming out of our servers' and shopkeepers' mouths, and they mine. In the most perfect twist of fate, the biggest communication breakdown of the entire trip was between Nathan and me. As it turns out, the person who understood me least, and whom I didn't understand myself, was sharing my bed just one pillow over.

Our first married fight was about money. I will spare you the details—they are mundane and trivial, as most domestic arguments are to outsiders. The argument was rooted in innocent miscommunication and misunderstanding, but the embarrassment, indignation, and confusion that welled up in me unleashed a torrent of fiery tears, stinging words, and large gestures, as if I were trying to wave away the crack that had begun its spidery crawl through our perfect five-day-old marriage. Within minutes, maybe even seconds, our own personal Tower of Babel was built, and to this day we are still working to tear it down. After that brief first argument came a moment of resignation, meaningful sighs, huffs, and mutterings as we packed to go home. Neither of us wanted to end our honeymoon angrily. Neither of us was anxious to carry the lonely ache of disappointment in ourselves and in each other home with us. We dispelled all ill feelings by the sweetness of rushed apologies and tender actions the rest of the day.

Still, the crack was there. A voice that spit out bitter seeds—*you really are alone, you really are misunderstood . . .*—took root in our marriage. To this day, money is still our number-one marital blister, although thanks to therapy, hard work, and the mellowing of age we have come a million miles in compassion and cooperation from where we were that last day of our honeymoon. But even as far as we have come, I would jump at the chance to go back and tell those two to slow down and listen and act from their hearts instead of their egos.

When I think of the Tower of Babel, I cannot help but also think of Pentecost, as they are both biblical accounts where a multitude of languages is a central part of the story. The stark difference between the two is that in the instance of the Tower of Babel, multiple languages are the tools used to confuse, divide, and scatter those who think they can reach godlike stature of their own accord, whereas in the occasion of Pentecost the variety of languages are the tools that are used to unite, order, and gather those who are seeking God to come closer to them. I find it interesting that the Holy Spirit moved in such a way that those first-century Christians had the ability to speak in various languages that the visiting Jews would understand, without any translation needed, instead of the other way around. Of course perhaps I am naive, to be surprised by this move of the Holy Spirit. Christ after all came to humanity, living as we live, speaking as we speak. But still, the thought is striking—the Holy Spirit did not come for the benefit of those on whom it fell, but for those whom they would encounter.

This must be why the Holy Spirit often comes like a mighty, rushing wind, a burning fire of conviction, blowing up my assumptions daily, telling me to walk beyond my experiences and understanding of the world, to meet people where they are, as they are—to listen and speak with an open and tender heart instead of an insecure and arrogant one, forsaking my comfort for the benefit of others, speaking in ways that they can understand, instead of the other way around.

Spicy Cajun Breakfast Casserole Recipe

What is it about breakfast casseroles that makes them so amazing? Next to those little meatballs cooked in grape jelly, the breakfast casserole may be my favorite southern party food. Nathan is partly Cajun, so I asked him to help me whip up a scrumptious breakfast dish flavored with a kick that would set our tongues (slightly) on fire. I bet after you have a bite you will want to kick off your shoes and start a right and proper *fais do-do*. Of course in Louisiana the dancing often begins after dark and the children have gone to bed, but why not go ahead and mix things up, start the day this way?

Ingredients

- 1 pound of bacon, cut into bite-size pieces, cooked crisp, and drained
- 1 pound of Andouille sausage, sliced into bite-size pieces, and browned in a skillet
- 1-pound bag of refrigerated hash browns (often found in the dairy section) with peppers and onions
- 6 eggs
- 1 cup milk
- 1 tablespoon Cajun seasoning
- 1 8-ounce package cream cheese
- 1½ cups shredded Colby Jack cheese (approximate)

Directions

Preheat the oven to 400 degrees.

Lightly butter a 9 x 13-inch glass or ceramic casserole dish.

Arrange the potatoes in the dish, then break the cream cheese up into cubes and stash randomly among potatoes

Place your cooked meat on top of this layer.

Next, in a separate bowl, mix the eggs, milk, and Cajun seasoning together.

Pour this mixture over the meat.

Top it all with shredded cheese.

Bake uncovered 35–45 minutes, or until a knife inserted into the middle comes out clean.

Let cool slightly before cutting.

If you prefer, you can prepare this dish the night before and bake it first thing in the morning.

Jamaican Hard Bread

When I visited the Bronx as a teenager, I stayed with a family friend who was originally from Jamaica. Shopping on Fordham Road with her, I was amazed by the complete melting pot of cultures, languages, and skin colors. I felt as if I had finally found America. After a long day of shopping, my friend bought us a loaf of the most delicious Jamaican hard bread. We stood at the kitchen counter, sliced into it, and proceeded to eat almost the whole loaf at once. I am pretty sure I gained five pounds over that weekend just from the bread alone. I have not been able to find the exact recipe, but this one is pretty close. Maybe if I ever get back to the Bronx I will discover the secret.

Ingredients

3   tablespoons sugar
1   package active dry yeast
     (0.25-ounce)
¾   cup warm water (110 degrees)
2   tablespoons vegetable oil
½   teaspoon salt
2¾ cups all-purpose flour

Directions

In a small bowl, dissolve yeast and sugar in warm water. Let stand about 10 minutes, until it appears milky.

In a large bowl, combine the yeast mixture with the oil, salt, and 1½ cups of the flour, stirring well. Mix in the remaining flour, ½ cup at a time, mixing rapidly after each addition.

When the dough comes together in a ball, place on a lightly floured surface and knead until smooth (about 8 minutes).

Lightly oil a large bowl (if you place the dough in a clear bowl, you will be able to better assess its growth) and place your dough in it, turning your ball of dough around in the bowl until it is well-coated with oil.

Cover with a damp cloth and let the dough rise in a warm place until doubled in volume, about 1–2 hours.

After dough has doubled in size, punch down the dough, deflating it.

Place deflated dough on a lightly floured surface and form into a loaf.

Place the loaf into a lightly greased 9 x 5-inch loaf pan and cover again with a damp cloth; let it rise for 1 hour.

Preheat the oven to 375 degrees.

Bake in preheated oven for about 30 minutes or until the top is golden brown.

Cool in pan 5 minutes and then turn out onto rack and cool completely.

Serve with large pats of cold butter.

Rhubarb Pepper Jelly

This jelly is a true melding of worlds. I spent my childhood in Alaska, where rhubarb grows plentifully, and I came to love all things rhubarby—pies, coffee cakes, you name it. When I moved back to Arkansas I discovered the joys of pepper jelly, and now, in the spirit of Pentecost Sunday, I have brought the two worlds together.

Prepare

To sterilize jelly jars, lids, and screw bands, begin by bathing them in hot soapy water; rinse with warm water and set aside to dry. Prepare your work surface. You will need a large-mouthed funnel, a pair of tongs, and at least 1 hot pad and 1 kitchen towel and 2 trivets to set the hot pans on.

Next, fill a small saucepan with ½ cup of water. Place on burner. Layer lid inserts, bottoms facing up in saucepan, and turn heat onto medium heat. When your pot of lids has begun to boil, you can remove it from the heat and place it near your washed and dried jars. You will need tongs to remove lids from the hot water individually when the time comes.

Ingredients

8   small to medium jalapeño peppers (stems and seeds removed), rinsed
1   small red or green bell pepper with seeds removed (optional)
4   cups chopped rhubarb stalks
¼   cup lemon juice
½   cup white vinegar
½   cup white grape juice
6   cups sugar
1 1.75-ounce box of dry pectin (I prefer Sure-Jell®)

Directions

Chop rhubarb into ½-inch-thick pieces.

Dice bell pepper into very small pieces and set aside.

Mince jalapeños using food processor (you should have about ½ cup of chopped jalapenos).

Add jalapenos and rhubarb to a large nonstick stock pot.

Over medium heat bring rhubarb and peppers to a boil, stirring continuously. (The water in the rhubarb will create a liquid that will boil.)

Cook until peppers and rhubarb are completely broken down, resembling the consistency of applesauce.

Add in liquid ingredients, bell pepper, and then pectin; bring back to a boil over high heat.

(Continue on the next page)

Quickly add sugar, stirring to dissolve.

Bring to a full, heavy, rolling boil and boil hard for 1 minute, stirring continuously.

Remove from heat; quickly skim off any foam.

Fill sterile jars, leaving ¼-inch headspace. Wipe jar rims and adjust lids and rings.

If the jelly is hot enough the lids will seal, but to be safe, immerse them in a hot water bath for 5 minutes.

Use tongs to carefully lift finished jars from water and let the jars rest on a towel until cool.

(If you are new to the canning process, I strongly suggest visiting the website PickYourOwn.Com, which has wonderful tips, conversion charts, and repair tricks for when things don't quite gel. In my experience jelly making is as temperamental as baking, and it never hurts to have a good resource to turn to for help.)

Corpus Christi

The Thursday Following Trinity Sunday

> All actual life is encounter.
> —Martin Buber,
> *The Martin Buber Reader*

For the majority of my life, my experience of Communion—the Lord's Supper, the Eucharist—was about as meaningful to me as eating my fiber bar and yogurt for breakfast each morning. "Familiarity breeds contempt" is the old adage, but in the case of Communion and me, I would say familiarity bred familiarity, which crowded out any hope for mystery. The blunt and embarrassing truth is that I did not feel a spark or any kind of holy moment when I took Communion. I drank the juice. I ate the bread. I sat back down. Sometimes I said a little prayer, but that is about all. The only feelings I had were those of chewing and swallowing, and then the guilt that came from believing that I should feel more: more holy, more reverent, more contrite, more something.

When I feel embarrassed or guilty, the first thing I like to do is to assign blame somewhere other than on my own head. The same is true for Communion and me. I blame my lack of attachment on being a preacher's kid—and a Southern

Baptist one at that. To a good Southern Baptist, there is not much room for mystery at the table of Our Lord, where the elements are only symbols of his body and blood and hold no mystical, transformative powers of their own. In the majority of churches I attended, the Lord's Supper was observed periodically, sometimes quarterly, hidden away during the Sunday night service—perhaps, in some of the churches we attended, in order to lower the risk of unworthy participants showing up. This sacrament was practiced so rarely that I didn't even realize there was a pattern or a rhythm to its appearance until I heard author Lisa Samson describe a similar experience.

If I thought anything at all on the subject while growing up, it was this: occasionally on a Sunday night, perhaps when they had run out of other things to do, the pastor and the deacons would decide to pass the silver platter that resembled a small hubcap, loaded with tiny glasses filled just to the brim with grape juice. (Of course, good Baptist girl that I was, when I saw a whiskey shot glass for the first time I thought that *they* looked like large Communion glasses, when in fact the opposite is true.) The first hubcap was quickly followed by a smaller, flatter version that contained small, square, puffy, pale crackers that tasted very similar to a stale oyster cracker minus the salt.

Later in my life I would learn that many of the hymns we sang in church were set to tunes sung in pubs and bars. This information combined with the tiny shot glasses and imitation oyster crackers was almost enough to convince me that the American evangelical version of church is just a bar dressed up in modest clothing. To compound this detachment was my insider knowledge that the juice we drank was stashed in the fridge in the church kitchen and that the crackers came out of a box kept in the upper cabinets. If at any point you found yourself starving mid-service you could always and easily go sneak yourself a snack. Taking the juice and bread as symbols four times a year was about as mystical to me as eating candy canes at Christmas and chocolate bunnies at Easter, no more, no less.

In addition to my Baptist rearing, I also experienced Communion at my maternal grandparents' Presbyterian church during holiday visits, where the elements were offered weekly. Real loaves of bread were passed, each member taking a pinch, followed by the ubiquitous and apparently interdenominational shot-glass tray. At the Catholic school where my grandmother taught, the Eucharist was altogether different. During Mass, members had to go to the front and have a wafer placed on their tongue, followed by taking a sip out of a cup that the priest held for them. I watched this ceremony with fascination and nervous self-awareness. I was half afraid someone would make me go up front, half afraid they wouldn't. I desperately wanted to see if this ritual would feel as different inside as it looked on the outside, but I never gained the courage to partake of the body and blood during these Catholic Masses, partially because my grandmother did not. Her reason was that as we were not Catholic it would have not been proper, and Maw, if nothing else, was and is indeed very proper.

As an adult, I and the Eucharist have had to find our way together, and I have primarily found connection to the Sunday morning ritual in my role as a pastor. As a key player in the holy pageant, breaking the bread and spilling the blood, a connection is easy to find. This experience is what Barbara Brown Taylor describes as being the "lightning rod, conducting all that heat and light not only from heaven to earth, but also from person to person." But sometimes this feels like a cop-out, like cheating, because deep down I know that serving the Eucharist and taking the Eucharist is not the same thing.

As a pastor I offered and shared the Lord's Supper each week with my church family. Somewhere along the way our small body of faith reached a compromise of sorts in how we, as a family, would approach the observance of the Eucharist, and so, through a blending of traditions and preferences, on most Sundays I would recite the words of a Mennonite hymn from the *Sing the Journey* songbook: "This is the table of our blessed redeemer, make no excuse, simply come, because around this table you will find your family. . . ." And they, my family of faith, in response would come. The young, the old, the broken, the healed. They would come in praise and they would come in sorrow. They would come in the knowing and in the questions. They would come to the table, where I would be holding out the bread; they would tear off a bite, dunking it first in the grape juice that fills a large clay goblet, then taking it into themselves, the essence of each morsel melting into their own bloodstreams. Christ in them. Christ in us.

Fully human myself (as if there were any doubt), I too come to the table to serve with a heart full of confessions, fears, hopes, humility, and brokenness. Sometimes I come with pride and arrogance. Sometimes I come in a rush, thinking of the next thing on my to-do list. Sometimes I am distracted by those who are walking through the doors of our little church as I am breaking the bread, but I continue on, I dig into the moment, sinking my heels into the carpet beneath my feet, grounding myself, the words pouring out of my mouth. "Come not because you have to, but because you need to. Not to prove that you are saved, but to seek the courage to follow wherever Christ might lead. Come not to speak, but to listen. Not to hear what is expected but to be open to the ways the spirit is moving among us."

I continue on and I spill his blood and offer the cup, inviting all who can hear these words to come to the table. And as they come I lean over to offer the elements. "Body of Christ, Blood of Christ," I whisper to them. I bend down toward the little ones, I lean in closer to the older ones who have trouble hearing or seeing. I look into their eyes, I whisper "I love you" to my husband, to my children, to my best friend.

I am offering a gift, the gift of mystery, thankfulness, and redemption—healing and praise. I smile and I give thanks in my heart, setting my feet firmly in the moment. Seeing only the faces before me, the face of Christ in those I love.

For me, the charge of energy is vastly different on the receiving side of the table, and more often than not my spiritual light is barely flickering as I take the bread and the blood into myself and walk back to my seat, feeling like an observer, not a participant. *Why do I only feel connected when I serve the elements?* I wonder silently. *Why is it so different? Is it this way for everyone except those who serve?* I know some of the answers to these questions. I know that I am not the only one who has ever felt this way. I am not that special. But at the same time I know that there are others who have had truly revolutionary experiences at the Lord's Table. I am sure it will not come as a shock if I confess that I am also often envious of those who have had tangible and transformative experiences while taking the Eucharist. In her book *Take This Bread,* author Sara Miles shares her experience of finding in one bite—in one gulp—redemption, fullness, and salvation. I am guilty of reading stories like hers with the hope of finding some sort of formula, hoping to beam some sort of holy insight into my anemic soul.

Several years ago, still recovering from a recent church meltdown, Nathan and I found a soft place to land in a large neighborhood church, a place where we could sit in the back pew and rest while our hearts mended. Eventually, after we had been there several months, we began to put our big toes in the water, serving in a variety of ways, building relationships. Nathan began to play with the worship team, and I helped lead a women's Bible study. Slowly the walls around my heart began to lower, and I felt myself open up to the hope that we would once again feel at home in a church family. Once a month this church family would gather to share a hot cooked meal and a night of singing and prayer, followed by the Lord's Supper.

It was during one of the once-a-month Wednesday night services that my faith worlds collided, as the worship leader from our previous church home (and one of Nathan's best friends) joined Nathan and other members from that band onstage. Singing familiar songs while standing elbow to elbow with new friends, I was overwhelmed by a sense of gratefulness for the crazy, winding path that my life had taken, a path that had landed me in that very room on that very night, participating in something so ancient—something that thousands of people have done for centuries—as Communion. So many threads of my story were woven together with the stories of all those who had gone before me and those who will come after me through this simple ritual.

Corpus Christi, also called the Day of Thanksgiving for the Institution of Holy Communion, is a day that the church has set aside to purposefully say thank you for the gift that is the ability to say thanks. For thanksgiving is what calls us into the moment, opening our eyes to what is in front of us. And thanksgiving, as Ann Voskamp brought home so beautifully in her book *One Thousand Gifts*, is the very root of the word *Eucharist*. *Eucharisto* means to give thanks, to be grateful, and so it follows that to live out the Eucharist, to be in communion, to be a part of the Lord's Supper, is to live a life of thanksgiving. But, as Voskamp says, *Eucharisto* is a "Greek word with a hard meaning that is harder yet to live." After all, it was with eyes wide open that Christ himself gave us this feast, this chance to come together and offer our thanksgiving; it was Christ himself who taught us what a gift the ability to offer thankfulness truly is. "On the night of Jesus's betrayal, he took the bread and he gave thanks"—these are words we have all heard in one form or another, words that I have spoken as I broke the bread. Here lies the root of faith. The root of choice. The root of the mystery that is the woven fabric of knowing, believing, choosing, trusting, and following. I read that passage and suddenly I can connect the dots between Christ's words and his reality; he gave thanks knowing he would be betrayed. He broke the bread knowing his body would break much more painfully, and still he gave thanks, and he told us to give thanks, and he told us to keep giving thanks *together*.

I realize only now that the reason I missed finding the connection on the receiving side of the table is that I have mistaken its meaning and its purpose. Christ's instructions were not to take, but to give. "Do this in remembrance of me. Eat this in memory of me." His directions are active, not passive. Do *this,* he says, and then he *gave* thanks (emphasis mine). We are commanded to take his body and his blood past our lips and into our body and our blood, accepting its nourishment. And we are not commanded to do this alone, but instead to offer our gifts of thanksgiving in the context of community—to come together, sharing in the same meal, the same body, the same blood.

Biscuits and Jelly

Unconventional as it may be, biscuits and jelly are simple everyday reminders to me of the Eucharist. Breaking biscuits open for my boys and passing the jelly down the breakfast table to my husband reminds me that we are to serve one another: not just at church, not just at homeless shelters, not just at work or at school; we are also to serve each other at home. Passing a platter of biscuits or a jar of jelly may not seem like much, but if it is done with a thankful heart, with a smile and kind word, these everyday actions can go a long way in showing our love for one another.

Granny Huffman's Southern Biscuits

These biscuits may be the reason I finally consented to marry my Sweet Man. His mother made them for me early in our courtship, and I have never looked back. The recipe has been handed down from Nathan's maternal grandmother, Granny Chevalier Huffman. Granny Huffman was raised in the Louisiana swampland of Catahoula Parish, and every recipe of hers that we make tastes just as you imagine God intended. I never had the chance to meet Granny, as she passed away before I met Nathan, but I feel that in her recipes I have a window through which I can catch glimpses of her spirit and her heart.

Ingredients

2 cups self-rising flour

4 tablespoons plus 2 teaspoons solid vegetable shortening or butter (The debate between shortening and butter in southern kitchens is long and contentious. Use whichever you prefer, but it is best to keep your preference to yourself.)

1 cup buttermilk

Directions

Preheat the oven to 425 degrees.

Add butter or shortening to baking dish (a 9-inch casserole or cast-iron skillet) and place in the oven to melt, while the oven preheats.

Sift flour into a separate mixing bowl.

Make a well in the center of the sifted flour.

Add buttermilk and 4 tablespoons of the melted butter or shortening (leave the remaining butter in the baking pan).

Mix ingredients together with a wooden spoon until a dough forms that can be worked with your hands.

Using floured hands, begin to knead the dough until the dough forms a ball in the palm of your hand.

On a lightly floured surface, roll dough out to a ¾-inch thickness and cut with a round biscuit cutter or cookie cutter (a small jelly jar works well, too).

Dip each cut biscuit in the melted butter or shortening that is left in the baking dish, making sure to coat both sides.

Do this with each cut biscuit, adding them to the dish as you go. The biscuits are best when they are cooked close together, so do not be afraid to crowd them.

Bake at 425 degrees for 15–20 minutes. Place biscuits under broiler on top rack for the last 4 minutes.

Let cool 5 minutes, then serve hot with butter and Cranny PomPom Jelly or honey.

Cranny PomPom Jelly

During our Alaska years my mother had a unique version of therapy—she spent many summer months picking berries, more berries than you can even imagine. She picked so many that she had to start making jams and jellies because our freezer ran out of room to hold them. It has been seventeen years since we lived in Juneau, and until two years ago we were still feasting on her currant and salmonberry jellies. Southern temperatures are too warm for currants and salmonberries, and berry picking in the hot Arkansas summers is not my favorite pastime, so I have started making my jellies from store-bought juices. I remember the first time I ate a pomegranate. I remember how beautiful the inside was, each seed suspended in a most perfect, ruby-red teardrop. I was instantly hooked. Pomegranates are a lot of work to eat for very little payoff, but their juice is so delicious I cannot resist. For this jelly I chose a cranberry pomegranate mixture because I loved the flavors and the color.

Ingredients

5   cups cranberry-pomegranate juice

7½ cups sugar

1   1.75-ounce box of dry pectin (I prefer Sure-Jell®)

½   cup lemon juice

Prepare

Wash jelly jars and screw bands in hot soapy water; rinse with warm water and set aside to dry. Prepare your work surface. You will need a large-mouthed funnel, a pair of tongs, and at least 1 hot pad and 1 kitchen towel and 2 trivets to set hot pots on.

Fill small saucepan with ½ cup of water. Place on burner. Layer lid inserts, bottoms facing up in saucepan, and turn heat onto medium heat. When your pot of lids has begun to boil, you can remove it from the heat and place it near your jars. You will need tongs to remove lids from the hot water one at a time.

Directions

In a large stockpot, pour juice and lemon juice together. Bring to a rolling boil, stirring to mix juices well.

Once you have a heavy rolling boil, stir in the pectin and ½ cup of the sugar. Stir quickly.

Once dissolved, add remaining sugar.

Return to full rolling boil and boil hard exactly 1 minute, stirring constantly.

Remove pot from heat and quickly skim off any foam with a metal spoon.

Finish

Move pot to work area where your jars are. Using a ladle and a large-mouthed funnel (found in the canning section at your local grocery store), transfer jelly mixture immediately into prepared dry jars.

Fill to within ½ inch of tops. Make sure no jelly gets on your jar rims.

Cover with sterilized lids. Screw bands tightly.

Jelly may be hot enough to seal your lids. Wait 1 hour to see if lids "pop."

If not, follow these instructions: Place jars on elevated rack in the bottom of stock pot or canning pot.

Cover jars by 1–2 inches with water. Cover; bring water to gentle boil.

Turn heat down slightly. Let boil gently for 5 minutes. Remove your jars and place upright on towel to cool.

Check seals by pressing middle of lid with finger. (If lid springs back, lid is not sealed and refrigeration is necessary to keep the jelly from spoiling.)

Let jars sit and cool for 24 hours before using.

Makes 6 1-cup jars of jelly.

(If you are new to the canning process I strongly suggest visiting the website PickYourOwn.Com, which has wonderful tips, conversion charts, and repair tricks for when things don't quite gel. In my experience jelly making is as temperamental as baking, and it never hurts to have a good resource to turn to for help.)

Grateful Mobile

Too often the ideals of gratefulness and thankfulness are set aside until the Thanksgiving holiday, when, truth be told, we often only take the time to put into words how grateful we are for the bigger blessings in our lives—our families, our homes, our health. But Christ did not instruct us to only give thanks for the obvious, nor did he instruct us to save our thanksgiving for major holidays. Instead we are to

let the peace of Christ keep you in tune with each other, in step with each other. None of this going off and doing your own thing. And cultivate thankfulness. Let the Word of Christ—the Message—have the run of the house. Give it plenty of room in your lives. Instruct and direct one another using good common sense. And sing, sing your hearts out to God! Let every detail in your lives—words, actions, whatever—be done in the name of the Master, Jesus, thanking God the Father every step of the way. (Colossians 3:15–17)

Recently, during a particularly fretful time, this point about "thanking God the Father every step of the way" was all too real for me. But both my mother and mother-in-law gently reminded me to thank God that he is in control even in the "lumpy times." That even when I am filled with "disappointment, anger, frustration, down-right boohooing," I must give thanks. I must still cultivate a grateful heart, and I must do so out loud. Out of this the Grateful Mobile was created. For our little family, this mobile is a way for all of us (and anyone who visits) to publicly share with one another and to declare out loud all that we are grateful for and in. Even the lumpier ones.

Materials Needed

- 15 mini craft clothespins (I found mine in the unpainted wood section of a large craft store; they are about 1 inch tall.)
- 30-gauge floral/craft wire
- 21 sheets of 4½ x 6½-inch scrapbook cardstock sheets in colorful patterns (These come in booklets at most craft stores. You could also cut your own sheets out of larger sheets of paper.)
- Lined notebook paper, cut into 5 x 3½-inch and 2½ x 3½-inch sheets (about 10 of each to start)
- Scissors
- 1 6-inch flat circular pressboard wreath form (found in the floral departments of most craft stores)
- 1 12-inch flat circular pressboard wreath form
- Assorted pens, markers, and crayons
- Craft paint
- Electric drill
- Glue stick

Directions

Your 12-inch wreath form should come with pre-drilled holes evenly spaced. If it does not, drill 8 holes evenly spaced and centered in your form, using a ³⁄₁₆-inch bit.

Drill four holes in the same pattern in your 6-inch wreath.

Paint both sides of your wreath forms twice, allowing the paint to dry thoroughly between coats.

Set aside.

Using a glue stick, glue together, back to back, 12 of your scrapbook rectangles. This will create 6 2-sided rectangles.

Fold the remaining rectangles in half and adhere with glue stick.

Next, cut 5 lengths of wire, 1 yard long each, 5 lengths of ¾ yard each, and 5 lengths ½ yard each.

Cut 4 lengths of wire, each 1½ yards long.

Use the 4 longest lengths of wire to secure your 2 wreath forms together as shown in diagram A in chapter 23.

Next, thread a length of wire through the metal circle in each of the clothespins. Twist the wire tightly to secure, and then begin threading each of these wires through the drilled holes, making sure to alternate lengths. (I hung 2 long ones from the middle, 3 shorts from the top wreath, and 10 from the larger wreath. See photo for example.)

To secure, wrap the end of the wire around the inside of the form and back through the same hole and twist the wires together.

Next clip 1 paper rectangle to each clothespin, remembering to alternate between large and small rectangles.

You have now created the base of your mobile.

Somewhere close to where you hang your mobile, keep a basket of markers, pens, and crayons along with your pre-cut slips of notebook paper. Invite your family, friends, and guests to depict—through words or drawings—what they are thankful *for* or thankful *in.*

Clip these words and works of art to your rectangles as they are created. Remember that this is a fluid project and should be updated and changed as often as needed. After all, gratefulness is not a one-time deal.

chapter 17

St. James's Day

150

Generally, by the time you are Real, most of your
hair has been loved off, and your eyes drop out
and you get loose in the joints and very shabby. But
these things don't matter at all, because once you
are Real you can't be ugly, except to people who don't
understand . . . once you are Real you can't become
unreal again. It lasts for always.
Margery Williams, *The Velveteen Rabbit:
Or, How Toys Become Real*

Today I am working on fading fabric, taking pieces of brand-new canvas in primary
colors and soaking them in a solution of water, bleach, and laundry detergent. Before
long it is obvious that different colors fade at different rates. The red fades so much
more quickly than the blue or the green, and the yellow fades so slowly that I am not
sure it has, until I empty the bucket and watch a gallon of sunshine run down the
sink drain. The process of fabric fading is one that requires much attention, despite
the careless look that I am trying to achieve. Each few minutes, I have to truck back
to the laundry room to make sure that each piece of fabric is stirred, turned, and
unfolded from itself while it soaks.

As is typical, I am juggling too many projects for one afternoon, and sometimes I let a piece sit in one position for too long, creating splotchy spots where the fabric, still folded together, didn't absorb enough of the bleach and is holding on to the original color. These uneven splotches resemble deep pigment birthmarks; it is obvious where their color comes from and where it was headed when it was so rudely interrupted. Finally my day consumes me, and I forget altogether, leaving a piece of canvas abandoned and forgotten like the dollar-store toys my kids bring home from birthday parties, which usually end up cracked and broken in the gravel of our driveway.

Late in the evening I clear the dinner table and take the dirty napkins to the laundry room, where I am confronted by my lapse. I peer hesitantly into my soaking bucket, surprised to see the fabric, a faded but still identifiable yellow. Some pigment is so attached to the fibers that it cannot be bleached out. The color is part of the threads, fused together beyond separation, despite my accidental attempt to rip them apart permanently. I stare into the bucket, down into the water, the yellow canvas fabric floating to the top. I dip my hand in the cool slippery water, draw the fabric up, wring it out, rinse it in the next bucket, wring it out again. I hold it to the light to see how much it has faded, trying to get a clear picture in the less-than-well-lit laundry room of just how much pigment is left, how far and how close we are to the original tint, looking for any dark patches that remain—any of the original color that was missed, folded over on itself, hidden from the pull of the bleach.

I have a deep affinity for faded things. Faded fabrics, faded papers, faded book covers, faded jeans, faded patinas on vintage icons found on the bottom shelf of flea markets. The sun-bleached, timeworn look of faded aprons and children's books. The chipped bowls and plates that I find one at a time at thrift stores. The old Fisher-Price toys I look for at garage sales, faded crepe paper streamers and honeycomb decorations I hunt down at church rummage sales. The leap is not far from the cracked and faded treasures that I collect to the cracked and tattered people that I love. Stirring the fabric, gently unfolding it from itself, I realize that most of the humans I love—my husband, my best friends, the kids at my school—also fit into this category. They are worn, broken, a little frayed around the edges. Even the writers I love most—Anne Lamott, Madeleine L'Engle, Kathleen Norris—are self-proclaimed broken things.

But this faded and frayed quality that I am drawn to in others and in the little treasures that I bring home does have a limit. Recently, during a particularly splotchy time, a time with more questions than answers, where my to-do list spun wildly out of control and the weight of the decisions and indecisions that I faced were drowning any hope I had, I felt covered in muck, as if I had wandered into a swamp dressed head-to-toe in denim and come out the other side, completely soaked through, my entire being weighted down, heavy and cold. This feeling was so uncomfortable, and I felt so exposed in my untidiness, that tears leaked out of my eyes at inopportune moments, anxiousness colored every conversation, and terse words shot from my lips before I realized what I was saying.

Sitting in a beautiful old stone chapel, waiting for a very popular author to speak, hoping to glean some sort of tidiness of spirit from him to set me right again, I realized suddenly that while I love the tattered and the frayed in others, I have no grace for it in myself. I expect perfection of spirit, to always be filled with brightness and buoyancy, to remain as crisp and unflappable as starched sheets. How impossible. Perhaps I am drawn to all the faded and used because in them I find hope that perhaps I could be loved that way too?

I prefer the authentically faded to what I am doing, forcing something that takes days, months, years to occur naturally to happen in minutes. Feeling guilty, and a little fraudulent in my attempt to make something look older than it is, even if it is just fabric for a project, I begin to think of James, son of Zebedee, a most faded and tattered apostle. As I am wringing out the fabric, transferring it from one tub of water to the next, I think of him sitting on the beach mending his nets, an ordinary fisherman on an ordinary day, doing an ordinary task. Christ comes to him and says, "Follow me, be with me, learn from me. . . ." (Matthew 4:18–22) and he does. He drops his net, he leaves his father, he leaves his job, and he follows Jesus, sand between his toes. He is not perfect; he is not like the flannel-board story disciples from my Sunday school days. Those disciples were always so neat and tidy, their robes starched, their hair brushed, their sandals polished. Instead James is a fisherman, which would be easily evident to anyone who sees him pass by. I imagine him looking more like the fishermen I knew growing up in Alaska than a storybook character. I see him as weathered, faded, with leathery skin, windburned cheeks, worn, calloused hands—a hardworking, authentic, honest-speaking man. A man who has no reason to follow Christ, other than that he was asked, and the question stirred something so deep in him that he had no other recourse than to answer with his life.

Laying my faded fabric out to dry, plumb worn-out and soaked to the bone with worry and stress, I cannot help but dream of being as sun-bleached as this fabric will be once it has hung on the clothesline to dry. I want to lie on a beach for days and days, allowing the hot, bright sun to penetrate my pores, drying up anything in me that is damp and at risk of mildew. I want all the bright spots, all the loud and brash parts of me, to be mellowed and aged. I want to be softened, not stiff. Pliable, not rigid. I don't want anyone to look at my life and think it is perfect or, worse, that I *want* them to think it is perfect. Instead, I want anything that is unapproachable or harsh in me to be scrubbed away by the salt and the sand,

revealing the imperfections, the brokenness, the cracks. Not because I am proud of those parts, but because I know that it is real. Like the Skin Horse and the Velveteen Rabbit, I am shabby because I live life, because I am loved, and because it is all work, it is all hard—living and loving and being loved, being transformed, being worn and faded. Here I am in my laundry room, wringing out my fabric, and even here Jesus comes to me and he asks, "Will you keep walking with me? Will you stay with me and learn from me and love me?" And all I have to answer with is my life.

Southern Summer Gathering

St. James is the patron of Spain, where his feast day is a national holiday. Over the years many traditions have sprung up around the legend that his remains are buried in Santiago de Compostela, Spain, and great pilgrimages have been made there. Many pilgrims began to wear badges or buttons made of different types of shells to show their dedication and pilgrimage. My southern take on this is to honor St. James with a low-country boil.

Low-Country Boil

Here in Arkansas we call this a crawfish boil, and it includes, well, crawfish instead of shrimp (as is the Carolina tradition). I have never really adjusted to the crawfish, their beady eyes staring at me, their bug-like tentacles stretching out at me, but I do love the one-pot wonder that is a boil. In England, oysters are the seafood of choice for St. James's day, and in France it is scallops. But again, they are not my favorite. For my St. James's celebration I prefer shrimp as my shellfish option, cooked with potatoes and cobs of corn—yummy, seasoned with the best spices—then dumped on a brown-paper-covered table to be shared by all. Because you can cook this all in one pot, this is an easy backyard or beach picnic meal to fix for a crowd.

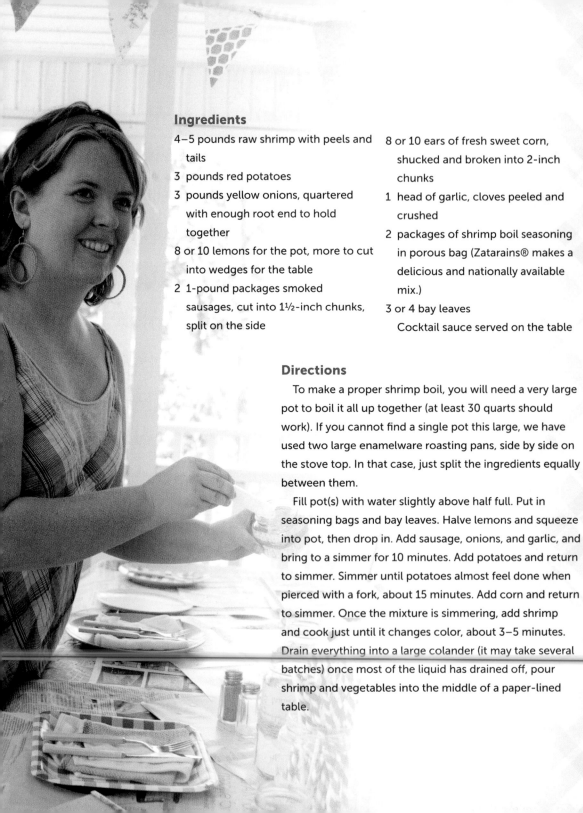

Ingredients

4–5 pounds raw shrimp with peels and tails

3 pounds red potatoes

3 pounds yellow onions, quartered with enough root end to hold together

8 or 10 lemons for the pot, more to cut into wedges for the table

2 1-pound packages smoked sausages, cut into 1½-inch chunks, split on the side

8 or 10 ears of fresh sweet corn, shucked and broken into 2-inch chunks

1 head of garlic, cloves peeled and crushed

2 packages of shrimp boil seasoning in porous bag (Zatarains® makes a delicious and nationally available mix.)

3 or 4 bay leaves

Cocktail sauce served on the table

Directions

To make a proper shrimp boil, you will need a very large pot to boil it all up together (at least 30 quarts should work). If you cannot find a single pot this large, we have used two large enamelware roasting pans, side by side on the stove top. In that case, just split the ingredients equally between them.

Fill pot(s) with water slightly above half full. Put in seasoning bags and bay leaves. Halve lemons and squeeze into pot, then drop in. Add sausage, onions, and garlic, and bring to a simmer for 10 minutes. Add potatoes and return to simmer. Simmer until potatoes almost feel done when pierced with a fork, about 15 minutes. Add corn and return to simmer. Once the mixture is simmering, add shrimp and cook just until it changes color, about 3–5 minutes. Drain everything into a large colander (it may take several batches) once most of the liquid has drained off, pour shrimp and vegetables into the middle of a paper-lined table.

Button-n-Shell Brooch

This button pin was inspired by the buttons and pins that those who make the pilgrimage to Santiago de Compostela in Spain wear. I thought it would be fun to make my own version for each party guest as a little memento. This is a simple craft that is not meant to be a long-term piece of jewelry, so do not expect it to hold up in the wash. Also, if you need a good party activity to keep older kids and teenagers engaged in the festivities, put them to work assembling these while you get the meal ready and the table set.

Materials Needed

- Photo Memory Button Pins (3½-inch clear plastic, 1 button per guest. These usually come in packs of 6.)
- Scrapbook papers in red, blues, and yellows
- 1 road map (it will be cut up)
- Hot glue sticks, hot glue gun
- Small seashells
- Colorful 1-inch flat-backed buttons (1 per pin)
- Ribbon in ⅞-inch width (I used grosgrain), 3 colors per button, cut into 5-inch strips
- Pencil
- Scissors

Directions

With your pencil, trace on your scrapbook papers and road map the circle shape of the button pin. Use the back piece of the button, face down, as your guide.

Cut out circles, place between front and back of button pin, right side facing up, and snap button together.

Using hot glue, adhere three ribbons to the back of the pin. Make sure to crisscross your ribbons so that they flare out.

Next, glue your flat 1-inch button to the center top of your pin, then adhere the shells around the edges of your pin.

Set aside to dry.

Hand your button pins out to guests as they arrive, or as they come to the table for the feast. You can also attach these to twine to make a simple napkin wrap.

157

A HOMEMADE YEAR **Summer**

chapter 18

Ordinary Time

> There must be more to life than having everything.
> —Maurice Sendak,
> *Higglety Pigglety Pop*

This summer I hung a laundry line in our backyard. Because I tied the rope up hastily and impulsively, the line is less than perfect. If I hang long or heavy things in the middle, they end up resting on the ground, collecting dirt along their hems. Had I been patient and let Nathan do the job for me, this would not be a problem, as he has a superior technique for doing just about everything (except doing things with expediency). So I took matters into my own hands. For some mystical reason, I needed to be able to hang laundry out to dry, almost more than I needed to breathe or eat. The impulse was that strong. Sounds ridiculous, I know. I blame Kathleen Norris, who I am pretty sure put the idea into my head when she wrote, "The ordinary activities I find most compatible with contemplation are walking, baking bread, and doing laundry," in *The Quotidian Mysteries: Laundry, Liturgy, and "Women's Work."*

159

ORDINARY TIME

Overwhelmed with my full-time job, my pastorate, my writing commitments, my roles as wife, mother, friend, sister, and daughter—all had taken some big emotional hits in the past year. My world seemed to be spiraling quickly out of control. My response to all of this was that I became a big mess of hot tears, frustrated outbursts, and too many hours hiding under my covers. The only thing that seemed to make sense to me, the only thing that I could muster any joy or motivation for, was hanging laundry. My laundry line was a place where my hands could be busy while my heart and my mind were set free. I could let loose my prayers, my questions, my rambling thoughts, my words, and give them over to God, letting him deal with untangling the mess I had made. So that is what I did, at dawn before work, at dusk before bed, and all day Saturday if I could work it out. Just me and the chickens, with the laundry and Jesus.

Hanging laundry on a line is a very ordinary task. It is as ordinary as scraped knees and lost keys, as fixing the same simple dish for supper again and again. Ordinary is most days, and Lord help us if we overlook them. More than the birthdays, the Christmases, or even the weekend excursions, our lives are made up of lots of commonplace events, routines, and demands. What is it the writer of Ecclesiastes said? "To everything there is a season." Sometimes the ordinary season can seem endless, and the beauty in it is hard to find.

Embracing the ordinary is something I have had to learn. I came into this world a little girl with very big ideas and no awareness that others did not share my vision for grandness. At nine I tried to throw a full-blown circus in our church gymnasium. For months I planned everything out. I talked about it ad nauseam. I made lists, sketched poster ideas, daydreamed about floor plans, and assigned jobs to all my family members. My father could be the ringmaster; my sister could walk the tightrope. All our friends' dogs could be in the show, with my brother teaching them tricks, like jumping through hula hoops. We would sell hot dogs, cotton candy, and caramel apples. We could charge a hefty admission. I was confident all our friends and church family would want to come and that this would indeed be the greatest show of all time. The only thing standing in my way between me and my vision was my mother. She could put up with a lot, but this was a bit too far.

My mother should win an award for ability to nurture creative children with the perfect mix of encouragement and restraint. In a bold and ingenious act of foresight, she pulled up all the carpets in our house to expose the vinyl school tiles underneath. Her reasoning? She wanted us to be able to paint and cut and glue and do all sorts of crazy creative things in our rooms without having to worry about it ruining the floor. My mother also let me draw a huge mural on one wall of my room that I never finished painting, and when I found a seven-feet-tall cloth palm tree at a garage sale, she was more than happy to cart it home, letting its palms stick out a back window the whole way. When I turned ten, by some fluke of fate, every girl I invited to my sleepover birthday party showed up. All twenty of them. Instead of panicking, running away, or calling the whole thing off, my mother, seven months pregnant with her fourth child, handled it with her usual aplomb. She made popcorn for all of us at midnight and pancakes at the crack of dawn, carrying on as if nothing unusual was happening at all. After all of that, even she had to put her foot down when it came to hosting a three-ring circus in the church gymnasium, and so my circus dreams faded to black.

The following year my father lost his job at that church, and our whole life went sideways for a bit. That year was the first year my mother homeschooled all of us kids. It was a year of never being certain of where the next paycheck was coming from, and of learning how to make boxed macaroni-and-cheese using only water instead of butter and milk. If my parents traded bitter, spiteful words, cried or yelled, threw dishes or cursed each other to hell and back, I never knew it. I never saw or heard them. Whatever marital negotiations occurred between my parents must have happened behind closed doors or late at night, away from my all-too-curious ears. Because while I knew things were tense, I never felt how precariously close they came to the edge, and I never felt as if our family unit itself were in jeopardy, just the state of our pantry. What I did notice, however, was how my mother suddenly took an active interest in gardening. Day after day, she would stand in the backyard watering and tending to her garden for hours at a time. I can still see her, standing there, hose in hand, stooped slightly over the garden, watering, watering, watering. Only now, standing at my laundry line, can I see that maybe it wasn't just about the garden at all. Perhaps there was more happening as she stood there, toes in the dirt, staring into the sunset.

Growth is never painless, and with each trip to my laundry line, my basket loaded with freshly washed items, I encounter evidence of my inadequacies. Inside the house I can shove laundry from one machine to another machine blissfully unaware of how bad things have gotten, but my laundry line is full of blunt truth. I pull one garment out of the basket at a time, pinning it to the line, and come face-to-face with each and every stain, every missing button, every rip, and every tear. The first time I pulled out a pair of shorts that I knew Miles had worn recently and realized they were two sizes too small and hung them next to a school shirt covered in stains, I burst into tears and confessed to myself what everyone else had been saying for months: it was time to decide how I wanted to live. The problem was never, as Shauna Niequist reminds me in her book *Bittersweet*, "deciding what I want my life to be about." What is hard, time and time again, is figuring out what I am willing to give up in order to do the things I really care about. Some days I have to keep going, keep juggling. But then come the days when I know I have to choose what to give up, what to lay on the altar and walk away from. This was one of those days. What I could no longer deny that day, looking at the brazen evidence of my neglect as a mother, was that I needed to choose—then and there—what to give up in order to move forward.

I finished taking the laundry down, went inside, and told my husband that I was ready to let go of my pastorate. Sitting on the couch, lying in his arms, tears surging forth, I knew all the way down to my toes that as hard as it was, this was what I had to do. I could no longer pretend that the extraordinary opportunity of being a female pastor would continue to suffice as an excuse for my missing the very ordinary moments of being a wife and mother. I had to let go of the idea that I was betraying my gender in making that choice. There are some women who can handle these demands amazingly well, but that morning, standing in my nightgown and boots, staring at a line full of ragged towels and too-small shorts, I humbly admitted to myself and to God that I was not that woman. At least not on that day, or in the foreseeable future. The time had come for me to choose the ordinary, to choose to enjoy my children and my husband, who it turns out are indeed my favorite people. To spend an ordinary Sunday morning sitting on my swing, sweet tea in hand, and listen to the birds and the breeze and the beating of my heart, without rushing off to the next activity.

Embracing the ordinary is something that even the church honors. Built into the liturgical year are seasons called Ordinary Time, a series of slow, repetitive, highly underscheduled days that bridge the more robust seasons of the church year together. Our entire planet spins and turns according to the rhythm of the sun, creating in every living organism a pattern of rest and work. In Genesis, God himself goes to the trouble to give us a pattern for our seven-day week, providing one day fully dedicated to rest. (And how many of us, myself included, have just turned that into another day of to-dos?)

Just as our own individual lives take on daily patterns and just as we have created a year-round rhythm by the annual repetition of birthdays, anniversaries, memorials, and vacations, the church year also follows suit. The liturgical calendar has created a pattern within our twelve-month rotation that provides for seasons of rejoicing, mourning, work, and rest. Perhaps the church forefathers and foremothers knew what modern Westerners would have a hard time admitting—that no one can sustain the intensity, activity, and emotion that Christmastide and Holy Week require for 365 days of a year. Everyone needs a break from even the most extraordinary moments in life, even followers of Christ. And so, built into the church year's rhythm is a time that calls us to stop, rest, and enjoy the everyday. A time to honor the simple and the ordinary, an open invitation to quiet, to stillness, to turn down the shouting of our busy modern lives, in order to once again hear our heartbeat and the heartbeat of God within us.

Children's Ordinary Day Party

The end of summer is a great time to throw an Ordinary Day party. After all, summer is about those most ordinary and wonderful experiences. Why not celebrate the simple gifts, the small and unimpressive, the ordinary and the lovely, and why not do it with childish abandon and joy? Of course, the temptation is there to work yourself to the bone to throw the perfect version of this party. But I would encourage you to take a step back and simply do what is fun—do not worry about matching napkins and plates, perfect invitations, and centerpieces. Use what you have on hand, what is simple and sweet, inexpensive and easy to put together. Without a doubt the best parties I have ever given have been the ones where I tossed caution to the wind and just had pure, ordinary fun.

Miles's Favorite BBQ Chicken Legs

My dad was not a big grilling guy. While I was growing up his version of cooking was cracking open a can of chili, a package of hot dogs, and a bag of corn chips on a Saturday. A decent weekend meal, but not exactly living high on the hog. When my baby sister Jemimah was born, I went and stayed with some of my parents' friends. For dinner they served what seemed like a mountain of BBQ chicken legs, straight off the grill. For years I dreamed of indulging in chicken legs like those again, but it wasn't until I married Nathan that my dreams came true. Miles loves BBQ legs as much as or more than I do (if that is possible), and so it is for him that this simple summertime dish has been named.

Ingredients

1 large package of chicken legs
1 shaker of BBQ Rub seasoning
   (Rendezvous is our preferred brand
   and can be ordered online.)
1 bottle of honey BBQ sauce
½ cup apple cider vinegar
½ cup molasses

Directions

You will need a two-level fire to grill the chicken legs. If you have a gas grill, turn half of the burners to high and half to low. If using charcoal, bank the coals to one side on the grill.

Two hours before you plan to grill (you can do this as early as 24 hours in advance), coat the legs fairly heavily with the BBQ rub on all sides. Cover and place in refrigerator.

In a mixing bowl combine half of the bottle of BBQ sauce, the vinegar, the molasses, and another tablespoon of the rub.

Once your grill is preheated, quickly cook the chicken legs on the high-heat side, charring them on all sides.

As you char the legs, move them to the lower-heat side.

Once all of the legs are on the low-heat side, baste with your sauce mixture and close the grill lid.

After 6 minutes, open the lid, turn the legs, baste again, and close the lid once more.

Continue turning and basting, every 6 minutes or so, keeping the lid closed as much as possible, until the chicken has cooked to well-done.

The key to yummy chicken legs is their "crispy on the outside, juicy on the inside" counterbalance. Getting the char just right and then allowing your legs to slow cook until done is the key component in this dish. This takes about 30–40 minutes in all.

ORDINARY TIME

Jolly Pops

Arkansas has especially long and hot summers, which means that baking goes completely out the window for the months of July, August, and even into early September. Ice pops are always a great hit with all ages. Little kids love them for the novelty, and big kids of all ages love them for their nostalgia. I have developed quite the repertoire of what I call Jolly Pops, which all include either instant pudding or flavored gelatin. They are sure to please any crowd, and they elevate the ice pop to party-worthy heights. Below is the recipe for the hands-down favorite for my boys, Ridge Road Pops, inspired by the flavors of Rocky Road ice cream.

You can make any of these in traditional freezer-pop molds, or you can do what I do and use small child-size cups from the dollar store and vintage flea markets. These little cups can also be given as party favors after the guests have enjoyed their Jolly Pops.

Ridge Road Pops

This is our family version of a Rocky Road–inspired ice pop, named after the street where these were invented.

You will need:

- 8 small plastic juice cups or waxed water-cooler cups
- 8 large wooden ice-pop sticks (also called craft sticks)
- 8 cupcake liners
- 1 large-mouth funnel

Directions

Line up your empty cups.

Cut slits into the middle of each cupcake liner and set aside.

In a cold bowl (I always put mine in the freezer for 10 minutes before I start), mix together pudding mix, 2 cups of milk, and 1 cup of whipped topping for 1 minute, till mixture thickens slightly.

Place your large-mouth funnel into your first plastic cup, fill cup ¼ with pudding mixture.

Add a sprinkling of nuts and chocolate chips.

On top of the nuts and chips, add 2 tablespoons whipped topping.

Top off with more chocolate pudding, filling your cup up in total ¾ full.

Insert wooden craft stick into middle of pudding mixture.

Invert the cupcake liner onto the plastic cup, letting the stick poke through the cupcake liner. (This serves as a sort of "cap" for the ice pops and helps them from getting freezer burn.)

Repeat this pattern with the remaining 7 cups.

Place all in the freezer for at least 6 hours.

To serve, simply take out of freezer and run hot water over the outside of the mold or cup, loosening the ice pop.

Ingredients

2 12-ounce packages of instant chocolate pudding mix

2 cups of frozen whipped topping, thawed

2 cups of milk

Toppings—chocolate chips, chopped walnuts or pecans, mini-marshmallows, Cool Whip, and sprinkles

167

Summary Pineapple Pasta Salad

his is an easy recipe that pleases many ages and taste buds. Cool and refreshing, it is also the perfect culinary foil to a hot summer day.

Ingredients

8 ounces of farfalle pasta (capellini and elbow macaroni are other good options), cooked al dente

2 tablespoons of honey

1 cup of pineapple chunks (fresh or canned)

1 cup of cubed mango (or you can double the pineapple)

4 fresh green onions, chopped

Juice of 1 large lemon

1 cup plain low-fat yogurt

1 tablespoon brown spicy mustard

1 teaspoon of dried tarragon

Salt and pepper to taste

Directions

Mix all the ingredients together and chill for 1–2 hours. This is one of those salads that is best served cold and well-soaked. If it dries out a bit while chilling, you can add a tablespoon of yogurt to bring the salad back to life.

Tin Can Bowling

This idea came about because we have some amazing friends who have given their hearts and their time to the homeless population in the central Arkansas area, through a ministry called The One, Inc. As a family, we collect recyclable aluminum cans to help put gas in the three vehicles that visit the camps loaded with supplies, food, and friendship almost daily. When we threw our Ordinary Time party we asked all our guests to bring aluminum cans to help this great ministry, but first we used the cans for a fun game of Tin Can Bowling.

Materials Needed

- Lots of empty, clean tin and aluminum cans in a variety of sizes
- Scrapbook papers cut in a variety of widths from 3 inches to 5 inches
- Clear tape
- Beach ball
- Piece of plywood or stiff cardboard, 3 x 4 feet

Directions

Wrap each can with a strip or two of colorful paper and secure with tape.

Stack your cans on top of your plywood or cardboard in a pyramid shape.

Let each party guest take turns bowling the large beach ball toward the can tower.

Allow smaller guests to stand closer for better results.

Let each player roll three times.

The person who knocks down the most cans in three rounds is the winner! (Dollar store beach balls make great prizes.)

Autumn

love

Tho' the storm and its fury break today,
Crushing hopes that we cherished so dear;
Storm and cloud will in time pass away,
The sun again will shine bright and clear.
Let us greet with a song of hope each day.
—Ada Blenkhorn, *Keep on the Sunny Side*

chapter 19

Holy Cross Day

Two months before Nathan and I were married, on an average Saturday morning in March, a tornado hit the small town where my family lived and where I attended college. The day of the storm, I was an hour away, with my maternal grandmother, Maw, and my younger sister Judea shopping for wedding supplies. What was originally just going to be a pit stop turned out to be providential when we stopped in to visit my paternal grandparents. Had we kept driving back home instead, we would have driven straight into the storm. As the skies darkened around us, we watched local news coverage, trying every few minutes to get in touch with my parents. The moment the meteorologist named my family's street as a devastated area, all I could think about was that I needed to keep it together, as I was stuck between two grandmothers and an eleven-year-old little sister who were all on the edge of their seats and their nerves.

173

Despite repeated attempts by several family members, no one could reach my parents on their one phone, an older portable model that stopped working every time the electricity went out. (This was before the age of cell phones being as ubiquitous as toilet paper in every home.) As I dialed their number over and over, I mentally berated my parents for their irresponsible behavior in not having a regular landline phone, no electricity needed. Being annoyed was better than being scared and felt a whole lot less helpless. I was eventually able to reach my future father -in-law, who lived one town over. Through sheer tenacity he was able to weave his way through the rubble of the neighborhoods hit the worst and arrived at my parents' home, working cell phone in hand, only to find their home destroyed and no signs of life. Standing near what was left of the house, dreading what might be buried underneath the rubble and the possible bad news he might have to deliver, he looked up in time to see my parents and my sixteen-year-old sister, Jemimah, walking down the street. They had gone to check on elderly neighbors and were returning to see what they could salvage before night.

Several more anxious hours would pass before we would be able to track down my nineteen-year-old brother. During the storm Joshua had been working at the small Piggly Wiggly® grocery store downtown. Initially posted in the parking lot to keep an eye on the storm, he finally went inside to help the other employees hide the patrons underneath the meat counter until it passed. All the windows of the Piggly Wiggly were blown out and the roof was damaged, as were most cars in the parking lot. Joshua would work the rest of the afternoon and well into the night moving truckload after truckload of perishable items to another store across town.

The next morning, before the sun was over the horizon, determined to get back home, Judea, Maw, and I made our way to Arkadelphia. As we drove south, we passed utility truck after utility truck from Texas, Louisiana, and Oklahoma headed north to the other storm-ravaged parts of our state. The whole interstate was one big parade of these trucks, one right after another as far as the eye could see. Somehow the sight felt strangely comforting. "The cavalry is coming!" I wanted to shout out. "Help is coming! I can see them!" I wanted to yell out to all those who were just waking up to the realities of destroyed homes and towns.

Over the next week we cleaned out the remains of the house, ate lunches in the soup tents that the Red Cross and other organizations provided, and we told and retold all the stories from that day. How my father, mother, and sister went into the closet in my parents' room. How my dad prayed the entire time, hearing what sounded like a freight train going overhead. How the one thing my mother had grabbed and taken into that closet was all the fabric for my bridesmaids' dresses. How the only portion of roof that remained intact was the little bit that stood directly over that closet. How the ceiling was gone too except for that one spot, and how all the things that had been in the attic above the closet were still sitting there, as if nothing had happened, as if angels were sitting in that very spot, protecting my family.

Over warm bowls of beef stew and hot cornbread, we heard about how after the storm had passed and everyone was safe and accounted for inside the Piggly Wiggly, my brother and employees of other stores took to the streets, along with local members of the National Guard, armed with cases of bottled water and peanut butter crackers in search of those trapped, injured, or in need of supplies. My brother told of the chilling fear that gripped him as he dug through rubble, afraid of what he might find. I told of how my grandmother, my sister, and I had taken the back roads to get home, avoiding the checkpoints that had been set up to keep looters and curiosity-seekers out. How brave and clever we felt as we pulled into town, never having been stopped once. All of us told and repeated these stories over and over, and we listened to all the other stories being told. Everyone in town had a story, a story of where they had been or not been. What they had seen, heard, felt, or done.

After two weeks the inevitable postdisaster rhythm of how a town restores itself took over, but during the first few days everyone moved in a series of fits and starts. The shock and disorientation of what we had collectively lived through could bring everything to a halt, and yet in the next moment the practical needs of cleaning up the wreckage, eating, drinking, and sleeping would prod us forward again, pushing us further down the path of recovery. Despite the put-one-foot-in-front-of-the-other, can-do attitude, the realities of the tornado's damage were still clearly evident. National Guardsmen set up camps on the corners of the streets and neighborhoods most affected. Sitting, three or four to a corner, around a small campfire, with guns slung over their shoulders to discourage looting, the Guardsmen would keep watchful vigils day and night, drinking from thermoses of coffee and canteens of clean water, the shadows of half-standing houses outlined behind them, lit only by the moon and their fires, all the electricity out for blocks.

During the day, rolling slowly down each battered street, the Red Cross van would come to visit—its bright red emblem of hope on a pristine white background in stark contrast to the dirty gray and now treeless neighborhoods. The popularity of the Red Cross van in those weeks could rival that of an ice cream man delivering free swirl cones on a hot summer day, but instead of sweet treats this van brought water, bandages, and most of all comfort and hope that all would be well again. Thinking back to those Red Cross vans and their emblem, I wonder if my life carries the markers of another cross meant to bring hope. I recall Elizabeth Gilbert in *Eat, Pray, Love* saying that "ruin is a gift. Ruin is the road to transformation." I am always struck by how true this is, how I can never circumvent the ruin part, no matter how hard I try. You cannot, after all, rebuild, restore, or revive something that has not yet been torn down, destroyed, or killed; but all too often I try to hide from the pain, gloss over the brokenness all around me. I would like to believe that I am not using Christ's cross to beat, berate, or condemn others, but if I am not using it instead to clothe the naked, feed the poor, care for the widows, adopt the orphans, and include the outcast, am I living out its message at all? To share the comfort and healing that Christ offers, I must be willing to go into the destroyed and damaged places in my community, my home, my church and face the ruin honestly, picking up one piece of rubble at a time, as we walk the road of transformation together.

The tornado of 1997 ruined many things in my family's life—it destroyed and damaged our house, cars, beds, dishes, plans, to-do lists, and to some degree our sense of safety. To this day, my sister Jemimah still makes everyone put on shoes at the first sign of a bad storm. But the tornado also brought about wonderful transformation. My parents' house was rebuilt, bigger and better, their daily lives transformed by the benefits of the relief that came after the destruction. Trust and mutual affection grew between Nathan and my parents, bringing them closer together as Nathan worked tirelessly to move all of their salvaged belongings across town before and after working long shifts as a line cook. And as corny as it sounds, all of us gained perspective about what really matters most in life, and none of us thought it was our stuff.

Red Cross–Inspired Appliqué Pocket Pillow

american pioneer Clara Barton started the American Red Cross in 1881 after she witnessed the good works being done by the Swiss-inspired International Red Cross. Having served in the Civil War, Barton was acutely aware of the needs that war creates, both during the fighting and after it has ended. The Red Cross symbol that we are all familiar with now was created so that Red Cross workers could identify themselves in hostile areas, sending a beacon of hope and help. This pillow can also be made as a gift to give to those who may need a reminder that they are not alone. The edges of the cross are frayed as a symbol that Christ does not ask that we come to him tidy and neat, perfectly pressed and finished; but that he wants us to come, just as we are, messy and lost, tattered and worn.

Materials Needed

- Main piece of fabric (I chose aqua gingham.)
- Contrasting fabrics in three colors (I chose a yellow polka-dot, a pink floral, and a red pin dot.)
- Pillow insert
- Thread
- Sewing machine
- Straight pins
- Hot iron

Directions

Begin by washing, drying, and ironing all your fabrics.

Next, cut the pillow fabric to measure 19 x 39 inches.

Cut Rectangle B out of the lighter color strip, measuring 5 x 11 inches.

Cut Rectangle A out of the darker strip, measuring 5 x 11½ inches.

To make the heart, use the pattern in chapter 23.

Creating the Appliqué

Lay the pillow fabric out lengthwise, right side down.

Fold the left side in 13 inches, press with iron, then open.

Repeat this on the right side, remembering to open after ironing.

This should create 3 13-inch sections, denoted by the pressed creases.

(The middle section will be the front of the pillow.)

Flip fabric right side up.

Center Rectangle A in the middle 13-inch section, horizontally.

Pin and topstitch ⅛ inch from raw edge on all 4 sides.

Lay Rectangle B on top of Rectangle A, vertically.

Pin and topstitch ⅛ inch from raw edge on all 4 sides.

Center heart sideways on the crossed rectangle, the top of the heart pointing to the left edge and the bottom pointing to the right edge.

Pin and topstitch ⅛ inch from raw edge. Remember you are leaving the edges of the heart raw.

For the Pillow Construction

Flip fabric wrong side up (your cross will now be face down).

Fold left edge in 2 inches, press, fold in 2 more inches, and press.

Do the same on the right side.

Stitch left fold down with 1½-inch seam allowance from outside edge.

Repeat on right fold.

Flip fabric right side up, heart cross facing up.

Fold right section in 9 inches (this will follow the original 13-inch crease).

Fold left section in 9 inches as well, overlapping the right section by 5 inches.

Pin and stitch the open ends with ½-inch seam allowance.

Turn your pillow sham inside out and insert pillow form.

Michaelmas

> Call it a clan, call it a network, call it a tribe, call it a family. Whatever you call it, whoever you are, you need one. You need one because you are human.
>
> —Jane Howard, *Families*

For almost four decades I have celebrated my birthday without knowing that it held any significance other than the fact that I share it with my uncle. I was thirty-six before I found out that I also share the day with Michael the Archangel and all the angels. September 29 is the day called Michaelmas. For the British, this is the day that marks the beginning of the fall school term. In some other parts of the world it is the day that the end of the harvest is celebrated. At Waldorf schools the day is a chance to play dress-up, with children dressing as medieval knights and dragons, reenacting good slaying evil once again.

As I am writing this, Michaelmas and my birthday are only days away. More than New Year's for me, my birthdays are about taking stock, about remembering the good, the bad, the ugly, and the miraculous. They are about giving thanks for the year past and giving thanks for the year to come. Drawing close to four decades of living as an earthling, I have come to a place where I am willing to believe in angels and dragons once again. The older I get, the more I appreciate the work of

181

St. Michael, even if my personal dragons have not been (and I pray will never be, God willing) of biblical proportions. This year, newly reacquainted with the story of Michael and his dragon, I remember the year the Dragon of Loneliness almost devoured me and how angels, in the form of a children's playgroup, slew him.

In the spring of 2007 my heart was broken, as 2006 had been a rough year from which I was not recovered. That year I had lost a job, started a business on shaky ground, lost a church, joined another (in body only), sent a sister off to a foreign land, moved a best friend to another town, and struggled to find my footing as a part-time working mother, leaving my children in the care of others, which I had sworn I would never do. Despite all my efforts, we still couldn't seem to get all our bills paid on time or in full, partly because we had bought a car we couldn't afford because of a *Field of Dreams* belief that if I bought it, the work to pay for it would come. Upon greater reflection I can see now that I bought the car because I wanted to do something, anything, to feel like I was moving forward, not backward—to prove to myself that things were getting better, not worse.

Compounding all of this was my experience of motherhood in community as being an increasingly lonely experience. Six years earlier, in typical impatient fashion, I had been the first of my close group of church friends to have a baby. While it was at times a very solitary existence to be the only mom in my close circle of friends, the experience was more like being a novelty, an exhibit at the fair. Everyone was curious and good-natured about the change in my life, but no one was interested in jumping into the lake of motherhood with me.

By the time I was pregnant with my second child, however, my best friends and acquaintances had finally taken the plunge. The pregnancies were so rampant at our church (there were twelve of us due within one month of each other in a church of three hundred) that the old joke about something being in the water started to

seem not so funny. The experience of being pregnant all together was a welcome change from going at it alone (although I felt bad for the onslaught of baby showers we released on our poor church family), and I looked forward to everyone finally understanding just what I had been going through for the past four years.

Not at all shockingly, things did not really go as I expected. My friends were adjusting and wrestling with the changing dynamics that a firstborn brings with it into the world—marriages, sleep patterns, and careers all hijacked—while I was adjusting to life with two kids. The shock for me was not how much work my second child was, which I had fully expected, but I was unprepared for how much work my first child continued to be. Nursing, diapering, and bouncing babies for hours on end is work in and of itself, but add to that a fairly strong-willed preschooler who still needs to be fed, dressed, disciplined, and cuddled and the emotional and physical workload can feel overwhelming—more so when operating on two or three hours of sleep. Instead of feeling the gap narrowing between myself and my friends, I only saw it widening. We had all become friends when we were either newly married or about to be, and our babies brought into focus the stark reality that who we were without kids was not necessarily who we would be with kids.

Before long I realized that although I loved my friends dearly, they did not parent like I did, and the differences, while truly insignificant in the long term, felt profoundly so in the short term. They bathed their children daily and sterilized their bottles, which they filled with breast milk they had pumped for hours while reading books with words like *wise* and *whisper* in the title. I on the other hand bathed my kids weekly, fed them things I had dropped on the floor, and looked to Anne Lamott's book *Operating Instructions* for parenting camaraderie. Everything from the way we dressed our kids, to the types of music we played for them, to the types of bottles we used became issues that could set us apart from each other.

The result of these changes was a restless discontentment stemming from the deep desire to be understood. I was lonely and wanted to stop feeling as if all of my decisions—from leaving our church to how I dressed my kids—needed to be defended or at the very least explained. Throughout that season it would be fair to say that I could be obnoxious in defense of the way we ran our little family. My loneliness and feelings of alienation were taking on the form of a dragon that would rear its fiery head and pour flames of judgment and condemnation on my friends and their choices. Even though I was painfully aware of this at the time, nothing I did could erase my loneliness or tame the dragon that only seemed to grow larger and fiercer as our children went from babies to toddlers to preschoolers. My heart ached. My desire was to be known and accepted, not just tolerated because of a general affection. Not just to be loved but to be truly understood. This desire only grew deeper with every change that we encountered during those early months of 2007.

I don't know if God commonly uses playgroups to slay dragons, but in my case he did. Despite my willingness to harbor and even feed the dragon that hid in my heart, God in heaven heard the true cries of my weary soul and in a bold act of merciful grace sent me a little cluster of earthly angels to rescue me. On one unassuming Wednesday afternoon he sent me Sarabeth and Alison and Natalie and Whitney (and Michelle, who would follow soon).

It was Whitney who invited me to the park. Alison greeted me with a wave and a smile. Sarabeth talked to me about the conflicts of being a working momma. Natalie kept me guessing with her long red curls, hippie skirts, and trio of golden-headed girls always trailing behind her. In each of them I saw bits and pieces of myself, the same bits and pieces that had felt so awkward and out of place in my other circles. These angels let their children play in the creek with no worries about bugs biting, muddy shoes, or scraped knees. There were multiple children in every family and a multitude of ages among them all, ranging from ten months to ten years. We sat on quilts and blankets, everyone opening plastic containers of fruits and leftover roasted chicken, passing bags of pretzels and popcorn. We ate organic crackers and Ruffles potato chips. No one made excuses or apologies for what they pulled out of their bags to share. There was no judgment for the organic or the processed. Whatever people had on hand is what we ate. The kids played. Babies were passed around. Sundresses, floppy hats, blue jeans, T-shirts, flip-flops, and hiking sandals were the uniforms.

Over the next few weeks, these Wednesday afternoon gatherings begin to soothe the lonesome ache in my heart, and I found myself looking forward to them more than any other gathering. As the weather grew too hot and then too cold, we moved our afternoon playdates indoors, taking turns hosting the motley crew of seventeen kids and twelve adults, planning dinners we could cook together, the host setting the theme for the menu—soup night, pizza night, and (my favorite) sushi night—all of us bringing the ingredients needed, each contributing what they could. Husbands arrived bringing in last-minute grocery store requests or additional kids home from piano or football or perhaps just coming home from work.

Once the kids had been fed, we adults would fill our plates and our wine glasses and plop onto chairs, sofas, floor pillows, wherever we could find a perch and eat our dinner, always delicious, always made in community. We sat together telling stories, catching each other up, always several conversations going at once, kids wandering in and out, flopping down beside us, babies needing to be rocked, and big kids with hurt feelings needing to be soothed. In these moments I was often the interloper, the one who had not been a part of the group for a lifetime. But I was happy to listen, to glean, to not be the one talking all the time, to observe, to just be.

Over time I noticed that when I was with my other friends, my friends from my prechildren life, I was no longer so threatened by our differences. The dragon no longer reared its fiery head as often or as fiercely. Its need to be validated and seen had diminished over time. For the playgroup angels had slayed that dragon just by their welcoming presence. They didn't do anything other than be themselves. They saved my life in that way, the way only the best of community experiences can. They saved me from the slow death of a shriveled heart that comes from too much inward looking, too much loneliness, too much feeling apart from others. They opened their hearts and their arms and their homes and allowed me to find myself there. To find myself at home among angels.

This spring marked five years since that first Wednesday afternoon. Our group now is made up of as many teenagers as little kids, and the variety of after-school events and the changing needs of kids who just keep growing is making it harder and harder to gather together as regularly as we once did. But every now and then we manage to pull it off, and when we do it is a beautiful thing. "The point of our crisis and calamities is not to frighten us or beat us into submission but to encourage us to change, to allow us to heal and grow," says Kathleen Norris in *The Cloister Walk* as she reflects on hearing the book of Revelation read aloud. The crisis and calamities of 2006 could have done me in, beaten me into submission, convinced me to accept life with the dragon as a permanent resident in my heart, because without him I feared that I would be swallowed up by the sadness and uncertainty that all the changes had brought. Instead, through the most ordinary everyday friendships, I was given the room I need to heal and grow into myself a little more, becoming a little more comfortable in my own skin and my choices. Sometimes Jesus comes himself to slay the dragons, and sometimes he sends his angels. This year on my birthday, Michaelmas, I will be saying a prayer of thanks for both.

Birthday Dinner

Because my birthday falls on the same day as Michaelmas, I wanted to throw a party for my own little group of angels on my back patio before the weather turned too cold. I chose the theme of doilies for the table settings and the decor, envisioning the doilies, new and old, as something like angels' wings. For the menu I drew on inspiration from the European Michaelmas celebrations, a date that traditionally was used as a way to mark the end of the summer harvest. These feasts often included a mixture of dishes that leaned heavily on late summer and early autumn produce, with roasted chicken being the main course.

Farmers' Market Savory Bread Pudding

Ingredients

1   zucchini, sliced about ¼-inch thick

1   yellow squash, sliced about ¼-inch thick (You can substitute eggplant for the squash if you prefer.)

½   cup of corn, frozen or fresh cut off the cob

3   cups of fresh kale (spinach will work in a pinch)

1   cup of diced red onion

3   garlic cloves, minced

3–5 tablespoons of olive oil

5   cups of day-old bread, cubed (My favorite is sourdough, but Italian and wheat work well too.)

1   tablespoon of chopped fresh basil, 1 tablespoon of chopped fresh parsley, and 1 tablespoon of chopped fresh sage
    or 2–3 tablespoons of Italian seasoning

½   cup of Italian cheese mix, shredded (or just mozzarella, if you prefer) and ½ cup of Swiss cheese, shredded, mixed together

2   cups of milk

6   eggs
    Salt and pepper to taste

½   cup of chopped walnuts

Directions

Preheat the oven to 350 degrees.

Grease 2-quart baking dish and set aside (or you can make this dish in an enamel cast-iron skillet from stovetop to oven).

Prepare vegetables.

Next cook all the veggies and garlic in olive oil over medium heat in a skillet.

Remove veggies from heat and stir in bread, seasonings, and ¾ cup of the mixed cheeses.

Transfer all of this to a well-greased baking dish or pan. Make sure the mixture is spread evenly in the dish.

In a separate bowl whisk together the milk (or for a richer dish use 1 cup of cream and 1 cup of milk) and eggs.

Add salt and pepper to taste.

Pour egg and milk over bread and veggie mixture.

Cover dish with remaining cheese mixture and chopped walnuts.

Bake, uncovered, for 35 minutes, or until a knife inserted in the middle comes out clean.

Let stand 10 minutes before serving.

Mug of Pie:
Brown Sugar Lemon Apple Pie

Some people are cake people and some are pie people—guess which category I fall into? I adore apple pie, especially with the tart taste of lemon added. This recipe is for individual portions, and when your guests are finished with their pies, you can wash and rinse the mugs and then send them home with your guests as a party favor. Or if your guests are too full after dinner for dessert, send them each home with a Mug of Pie as a bedtime treat.

For this recipe you will need 16 small coffee mugs that are ovenproof (or 1-cup jelly jars). I purchased all of mine at a local thrift store.

Filling

10   Granny Smith apples, peeled and cubed
6   Gala apples, peeled and cubed
     Juice of 2 lemons, zest of 1 lemon
2   teaspoons of pure vanilla
1   cup of brown sugar
2   teaspoons of sea salt or 1 teaspoon of table salt
1   stick of salted butter, chilled and diced

Crust

2½   cups of flour
2   sticks (½ cup) of butter, chilled and diced
1   teaspoon sea salt
4   tablespoons of ice water (You may have to use more or less depending on how humid the weather is.)
1   lightly beaten egg for brushing on crusts

Directions

Make your crust first, as it will need to chill for at least one hour.

Mix butter and dry ingredients in food processor or with a pastry cutter until the mixture resembles coarse meal.

Pulsing the food processor, add 1 tablespoon of ice-cold water at a time until the dough comes together in a smooth ball. You can do the same by hand.

Wrap the dough in wax paper or plastic wrap and chill.

Next, prepare your apples, and then mix them with the remaining ingredients (except the butter, which you will add after cups are filled) in a large bowl.

Chill the apple mixture while you prepare your mugs.

You will need 1 smaller circle of dough for the bottom of your mug and 1 larger circle for the top.

Roll out your dough and cut out 32 circles, 16 smaller and 16 larger, using biscuit cutters or additional cups in the right sizes. Place a small circle of dough in the bottom of each mug and then fill with apple mixture.

189

Make sure to fill each just above the rim of the mug, as the apples will cook down.

Place 2–3 small pats of butter on the tops of each mug of apples.

Next, top mugs with the larger circle of dough, pinching the edges down around the rim of the mug.

You can prepare these mugs in advance of a party and keep them in the refrigerator for up to 2 days.

Preheat the oven to 425 degrees.

When you are ready to cook the pies, brush tops of pies with egg wash and place them on cookie sheets, 8 mugs to a pan.

Bake for 15 minutes, then rotate cookie sheet 180 degrees.

Bake pies approximately 15 more minutes or until they are bubbling in the center, with golden crust on top.

Let cool 10 minutes.

Serve with a small scoop of vanilla ice cream on top and adorn with pie flags.

Pie Flags

These little flags are cute, easy to make, and the perfect addition to a mug or slice of pie for any occasion.

Materials Needed
- Toothpicks
- White or colorful cardstock paper
- Printer
- Scissors
- Glue (craft and glue stick)

Directions

Copy or print the Pie Flag patterns found in chapter 23 on cardstock paper.

Carefully cut out the flags, making sure to not cut the crease where the two sides of each flag are joined.

Fold each flag along the crease and open flat.

Add a very thin bead of glue along the inside crease.

Place toothpick in fold of crease, half the way up.

Add another bead of glue or use glue stick along the edges of flag.

Fold and press closed.

Let dry.

191

GranMary's Angel Rolls

These rolls are as light and airy in texture as the wings of angel, which is how they got their name. My mother-in-law makes these for special occasions and large family gatherings because you can make the dough ahead of time in large batches and then cook on demand.

Ingredients

5   cups of unsifted flour
¼   cup of sugar
3   teaspoons of baking powder
1   teaspoon of salt
1   teaspoon of baking soda
½   cup of sunflower or canola oil
1   package of dried yeast, dissolved in
    2 tablespoons of warm water
2½ cups of buttermilk

Directions for Dough

In a large mixing bowl, sift all dry ingredients together.

Next mix in liquid ingredients, including yeast mixture, stirring by hand until dough forms .

Let dough rise one hour in a warm, draft-free place.

Punch dough down in center to deflate.

Store in airtight container in refrigerator until ready to bake.

To Bake

Preheat the oven to 425 degrees.

Grease bottom and sides of 9 x 13-inch glass baking dish and set aside.

On a lightly floured surface, roll dough out to ½-inch thickness.

Cut dough with a 2½-inch biscuit cutter and place in baking dish, allowing edges of rolls to touch. (You will not have to let dough rise again before baking.)

Bake until rolls are golden, about 10–12 minutes depending on your oven.

Vintage Harvest Bunting

have a weakness for decorative buntings and banners. I love to string them up everywhere for no particular reason, all year long. For years I have collected vintage handkerchiefs and doilies, and occasionally I pull them out and find a way to display them for a week or maybe a month, but the majority of the time they have just lived stuffed in drawers, hidden from view. For this party I decided the time had come to use my hankies and doilies to create a party bunting, fluttering with my most favorite hankies.

Materials Needed

- Quantity of vintage or new doilies and ladies' handkerchiefs, approximately 24
- Sufficient grosgrain ribbon (¾ inches wide) to stretch across your bunting area
- Sewing needle and thread

Directions

Measure the area you want to hang your buntings on. (I made 2, each 8 yards long because I wanted them to make a big impact in the outdoor space.)

Cut your ribbon to the length (or lengths) of the area you just measured.

Next, gather your hankies and doilies. Cut medium and large doilies in half. (I have not found that the edges of mine fray. I don't wash them, but you could always use a product such as Fray-Chek on the edges if you are concerned about them unraveling.)

Next, stretch your ribbon out across a long flat surface. (I used my living room floor.)

Alternating colors, patterns, and styles, arrange your hankies and doilies along your ribbon, leaving about 1 inch in between each item.

Once you have placed your hankies and doilies and you are happy with your pattern, pin each one to your ribbon. Finish by sewing your hankies to your ribbon with a simple topstitch.

MICHAELMAS

All Saints' Day

Pick up a needle and thread, and stitch together something particular and honest and beautiful, because we need it. I need it.
—Shauna Niequest,
Cold Tangerines

nd All Souls' Day

In Mexico, there is a belief that humans die three deaths; first, when your spirit leaves your earthly body; second, when your physical remains are lowered into the earth; third, when your memory has been forgotten. Perhaps vanity has a hand in this for me, because the third one makes the hair at the back of my neck stand at attention. I do *not* want to be forgotten. At least not by those who love me and know me—I am accepting of the fact that the world at large eventually will forget me. Eventually my writings, my art, and my contributions to society will all fade and slip quietly away, as they should. But perhaps, for at least a few generations, those who know and love me will keep this third death at bay. Perhaps those who know and love me best will stitch my story to theirs, cook a few of my recipes, save a few of my handmade pillows, and laugh at more than a few of my eccentricities. They may remember (or even share) my phobias (math, competitive activities), my preferences (one foot kicked out from under the covers when I sleep, spiral-bound notebooks for journal-writing), and my afflictions (withered pinkie toe, inability to say no to bacon, tendency toward anthropomorphism).

This last affliction, which has been passed on to me by my mother, is the one that seems to get me in the most trouble. It is this peculiarity of character that I blame for all my overflowing closets, for my jam-packed kitchen cupboards, and for having enough vintage plates to serve dinner to Napoleon's army. When I walk through a flea market or an estate sale, I am powerless to the pitiful, tattered vintage

195

pincushion whose colors are so perfectly faded. "I am at least useful!" she calls out to me in a huff, as I try to walk past her. The sad, one-eyed rag doll, the lonely aqua blue plate, the fraying copy of *Little Women*—they all speak to me. I *know* that if I leave them and walk away, they will end up buried under waste and filth at the garbage dump. "I am doing my part to save the planet!" I decree when Nathan rolls his eyes at my latest rescue. This strange affliction of mine is how I came to own a quilt topper full of the names of women I do not know.

The quilt topper is a pieced-together work of art. Each quilt square contains the hand-stitched name of a different woman, each square unique in its choice of fabric and pattern. How it came to be, why it was never finished into a quilt, and for whom it was intended are questions that I can only solve through pure imagination. There are a few clues for the serious investigator: the names, the date 1936, and the word *demonstrator* under one of the names. Was the quilt a gift for a friend moving far away? Perhaps they are the names of members of a sewing circle, a quilting bee, a Bible study, a sorority, or a home economics class? Whatever their story, whoever they are, I could not leave them at the estate sale where I found them, where they would surely be passed over, left for the donation pile or perhaps the trash bin. After all, who wants a quilt with the names of perfect strangers written all over it? Me. That's who.

I found the quilt topper a few months after my friend Tricia began inviting a small group of women from our church over to her house for monthly gatherings. Despite our occasional efforts to get organized and read a book or tackle a project together, the truth was that those gatherings were a lifeboat that we could all climb in together, in whatever condition we found ourselves—wounded, angry, hopeful— and begin to unpack and process what was happening to our family of faith. The community where we had all met, which many of us had married in, dedicated our babies in, and worked tirelessly for, was now disintegrating in front of us despite all of our best efforts to put it back together again. The changes that were happening were beyond our control and, as worn and tired mothers of small children, we were at a loss for how to fix the crumbling community when we were daily trying to figure out how to fix our marriages, our bank accounts, and our completely shattered sense of self that all too often comes with new motherhood.

We named ourselves the St. Zita Sisterhood after the thirteenth-century St. Zita of Lucca, who is the patron saint of lost keys. Young mothers—some working, some staying at home, some working from home—we were all a bit frazzled. Our hearts, emotions, and minds resembled pizza dough that had been pulled and tugged too much, long stretchy holes emerging in the thin places. Losing our keys often was something all of us could identify with, no matter how we spent our days. An old skeleton key became our symbol, and in each other we hoped to find a way to unlock the confusion we felt over what was happening at church, what was happening in our marriages, with our children, and in our own hearts as we confronted the reality that life does not often turn out as planned. The Zitas are the reason I bought the quilt topper with all the strange names. That could be us, I thought, holding the topper up to the light, standing in a small bedroom at an estate sale. I knew that the names, all stitched together, all different, were somehow part of the same story. I couldn't help but wonder what the story was—if any of them remained friends over the course of their lifetimes. If they knew each other's secrets and wiped away each other's tears. If they had fought, if they had made up. Were they like my Zitas?

Over the past decade of meeting and gathering, a lot has happened to our small circle. As a group we have experienced adultery, divorce, miscarriages, bankruptcy, moves to foreign countries and back again, surprise pregnancies, adoption, children with special needs, and many, many lost keys. There have been times when one or more of us has climbed out of the Zita lifeboat and into another or jumped back into the ocean to risk finding our own way alone. Even as I write this, it has been several months since we had an official gathering of the Zita Sisterhood, and it has been over a year since all ten of us have found ourselves in the same room. At times it is hard to be all together, our differences becoming more pronounced as we age. Our friendships, woven together during a time of heartache, have experienced growing pains as our healing has come in different ways, at different speeds, often going in different directions. I confess that at times I have been the one to jump ship solo, looking to make my own way, to wrestle with my insecurities, questions, and shortcomings.

Nathan and I are thinking of downsizing—of buying a smaller house on a larger plot of land—and this move will mean that I have to let go of so many of my thrifted treasures. Rag dolls, and multiple copies of *Little Women*, and more will have to be offered up to other loving homes in a garage sale. But the quilt topper will stay and travel with me wherever we go, because despite my all-too-often petty heart, and my solo wanderings, I cannot deny that the Zitas are my sisters. Our lives are stitched together forever, through our memories and the stories we tell, and the stories we are living. They are the women who sat with me while I cried salty tears, my heart broken over the loss of relationships I thought would last forever. These are the women who can tell the stories of my pregnancies, the demise of my small business, and of my love affair with coffee as well as I can. To borrow a line from the radio host Bernard Meltzer, they are the ones who know the song in my heart and can sing it back to me when I have forgotten the words. I would not be who I am if their stories were not stitched to mine.

All Saints' Day and All Souls' Day are the days to sing the songs back to those who have forgotten, and to sing the songs of those who may be forgotten if we do not do our part to keep their memory alive. These are the days that we set aside to tell stories of faith, hope, and sacrifice, stories that have been passed down to us through our biological families, faith families, or chosen families. These are the days to connect the dots between their lives and ours and the ones to come. To talk and remember where we have come from, to honor those who paved the way through heartbreaks of their own, to say thank you to those who helped heal ours. Human history is vast, our stories deep and spread out, the roots tunneling through time back to the beginning. As human beings, we are connected to each other through genetics, through common experiences, and through the one story we are all participating in. When we tell our stories, when we read from the Scriptures, when we study the history of our faith, we are unfolding the crazy quilt of the Story of God. A beautiful, intricate, pieced-together-one-scrap-at-a-time quilt. No matter how jagged or ragged the pieces we add, no matter how uneven or precious or dirty, a beautiful design continues to emerge.

Over time our stories become memories, and each memory is connected to another and then another and then another, the pattern reaching as far back as the day of Creation. You and I are living stories that will inform and influence the lives and the memories of those all around us, and it is the sharing, telling, hearing, and understanding of each other's stories that will "make us more alive, more human, more courageous, more loving," as Madeleine L'Engle so perfectly articulated in a 1991 radio program called "The Mythical Bible."

This is how I find meaning in All Saints' Day and All Souls' Day. I am reminded that every day I have the chance to pick up a needle and some thread and add to the story. To stitch together something beautiful and unique, to patch a small scrap of fabric to the story, to the Story of God, that will be retold again and again for all of eternity.

Patchwork Wreath for Autumn

The wreath represents the circle of life, and the scraps of the fabric represent the individuality of each of us. The fabrics overlap, representing how each human life affects another, a reminder that no one is an island, all our stories are connected, stitched together. The wreath is topped off with a flower to represent the beauty that comes from this wonderful connection to each other, to our history, and to our faith.

Materials Needed

- 12-inch foam wreath (I chose one that was white and had a squared-off edge, instead of rounded.)
- 17 strips of fabric in a variety of patterns, cut with pinking shears to measure 2½ x 7 inches (I used patterns in aqua, red, lime, yellow, and chocolate.)
- 34 straight pins
- Needle
- Thread or embroidery floss
- 1 button
- 1 large vintage crochet flower (I cut mine from vintage doilies), or 1 handmade felt flower, or 1 silk flower in fall colors
- 2 vintage crochet leaves cut from a doily (You could also cut leaves out of green felt.)

- 1 circle, cut with pinking shears out of a sturdy twill-like fabric, a bit larger than the diameter of your flower

Directions

Cut all 17 of your strips of fabric and lay aside. Press if wrinkled.

Next, using your needle and thread, sew together your flower. Build your flower in this order, like a pizza: first the circle base, next the leaves, followed by the flower.

Using needle and thread (I prefer two strands of embroidery floss), sew these three layers together. Once the base, leaves, and flower are secure, add the button in the center of the flower. Set aside.

Now you can wrap your wreath. Pick your first strip of fabric and wrap it around the foam wreath, securing both ends on the backside of the wreath with straight pins. (I prefer to use straight pins rather than hot glue or double-stick tape because it allows me to make adjustments as I go.) If the back of your wreath is going to be visible, you can go back with a hot glue gun after your wreath is complete and replace the pins with dots of glue.

Next, going clockwise, add your next strip of fabric, layering it about ¼–½ inch over the previous fabric. Continue this process with the remaining strips until your wreath is covered.

Add your flower, securing with two more straight pins or a lovely vintage hat pin, and hang the wreath on your front door, over a mirror, or on your mantel for a little patchwork quilt charm.

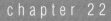

chapter 22

Christ the King Sunday

"When you take the small roads you see the life that goes on there, and this makes your own life larger."
—Elizabeth Berg,
The Pull of the Moon

The Sunday
Before the First
Sunday in Advent

For a brief time in the late summer of 1995 I was engaged to someone other than Nathan. Engagement may even be too strong a word because there was no ring and, upon reflection, there was not much love. But I will allow the term to stand because of two things: first, he did ask my father for my hand; and second, my best friend from high school, Tracy, bought a ticket to come from Alaska to Arkansas for the week that would have been my wedding week—the week of Thanksgiving.

Growing up in Juneau, my social life had two things working against it besides my general oddities—I was homeschooled for the majority of our time there, and our church was fairly small. However, a brief stint in the public school system resulted in my making two bosom buddies for life: Carrie McMillian and Tracy Lingle. Over the years, Tracy and I have been good at keeping in touch, while Carrie and I have a spottier history, with long gaps. But somehow the three of us have always managed to reconnect just when it is most needed. That autumn, with Tracy's arrival only days away and my wedding off the agenda, I suddenly had the urge to find Carrie, to let her know that Tracy would be in the lower forty-eight states. Carrie, who was a student at the University of Georgia, bought a plane ticket without hesitation to Arkansas.

Suddenly we three were together again. We were in a small southern town with nothing on our hands but time. Someone piped up with the idea that we should all hop in my 1976 Plymouth Volare and drive to Memphis to visit Graceland. I thought it was about the craziest idea I had ever heard, but both Tracy and Carrie seemed excited and I was quickly outvoted. Even my mother, whom I was counting on for sensible and reasonable advice, thought it was a great idea. "You'll be fine!" She encouraged us. "The three of you together will be safe—go, have fun!" That was all Carrie and Tracy needed to hear. The proverbial deal was sealed and the morning of Black Friday found us, fortified with Maw's amazing whole-grain waffles, headed to Graceland.

When I was four years old my family moved to Memphis so that my dad could attend seminary. Elvis had died only a year earlier and our apartment complex was right down the street from Graceland. Despite all this, I only have one memory that is Elvis-specific from those years. My mother and I were in the car, slowed in traffic. I saw a billboard that had Elvis's picture on it, and I was able to read the words "The King." I asked my mother—who is Elvis and why is he the king? My mother, who is notorious for her no-nonsense approach, replied, "He was a famous man who died from drugs. But he is not king, only Jesus is king." By the time Tracy, Carrie, and I found ourselves at Graceland, I knew a lot more than what my mother had said all those years ago. I had learned that my great-great-aunt had delivered baby Elvis in Tupelo, Mississippi. I had met his stepbrother Randy Stanley, who had done some traveling and preaching with my uncles when I was in junior high. I had read some biographies, I had watched movies and documentaries, and I was familiar with the roller coaster that was Elvis's life. Now after all these years I was going back to Memphis, and I was going to Graceland, land of Elvis the King, to see his trophies and his crowns, to walk through the gates of his kingdom, to gape at his image on everything from toothbrushes to area rugs.

Icons of Elvis have never been my thing, but I do have a weakness for Mary and Jesus: pictures, prayer cards, statues, and candles. I prefer items that are painted my favorite colors of aqua and red, and paintings and objects that are faded, frayed, vintage. Nothing shiny, please. My favorite from my small collection is an old plaster altar with Jesus and Mary standing side by side, a little space between them for a candle and a small bundle of flowers. The colors are chipped and worn away; Mary and Jesus each hold their hands to their hearts, each of their faces serene, reflective as if they are on the cusp of whispering loving words to me. Mary looks more concerned, which is only right as she is the mother, and mothers are always concerned. There is a diagonal crack between Jesus and Mary. Despite the efforts of a former owner to paste it together, the crack is obvious and cannot be missed. I like the crack. It looks familiar, identifiable. *Oh yes,* I think. *I have that crack too. Right in the middle.* In truth sometimes I like the crack too much; it becomes my idol. I point at it, show it off, and say things like, "See, this is what makes me different, special, unlovable. This is what separates me from you." I point it out to Christ, as if he doesn't know it is there. "See," I say, "this is what keeps me from you. This crack.

If you would take the crack away, well, then I could serve you fully, wholly, easily. It's this crack that holds me back. Do something about it."

Standing in the Graceland gift shop, I thought about the cracks in Elvis. How all the images of him, on soap dispensers, diaper bags, and oven mitts, are all so shiny. Young, healthy, happy Elvis is obviously the big seller. There is no place for older, worn-down, overweight, sweaty, sad Elvis here.

After we had toured all of Graceland we could afford (the airplane and cars cost extra to see) and dropped a few coins in the gift-shop offering plate, we headed to Beale Street. After a hot and fortifying dinner of red beans and rice, we quickly saw all of Beale Street that we could, since we were underage, and hurriedly walked back to the car, cutting through small side streets, away from the jarring lights and bustle, as the temperature was dropping quickly. As we headed to our car, a small jittery man stopped us and asked us for money. I cannot remember if he gave us a reason for asking, but I do remember that Carrie, without a moment's hesitation, without an ounce of fear, pulled out some bills to give him and wished him well. "Why not?" she said when Tracy and I looked at her inquisitively as we all headed back to the car, my mind swirling with what I had just seen. Someone well off the beaten and approved path had asked for help and my friend had given it, no questions asked, no hesitation, no lecture given, no strings attached. She didn't even seem particularly worried about what he might do with the two dollars. He asked. She gave.

On the two-hour drive back home, tired and cold, we all argued about something, probably something broad like "Does God Exist?" or "Is There Only One Person for Each of Us?" For years afterward I felt bad about this argument, mostly because as I remembered it, my role was that of the total, obnoxious bully, completely unwilling to bend, self-righteous in all my opinions. Years later, when we were together again for Tracy's wedding, I apologized for my complete lack of love and humility during that ride home. To my surprise neither Carrie nor Tracy remembered the argument as darkly as I did, and, despite years of my worrying about it, that ride home had not in any way clouded their opinion of me or their memories of that trip. Apparently they knew and loved me despite my flaws, my imperfections, my know-it-all tendencies. The massive crack running down the middle of me did not scare them off, did not surprise them, did not cause them to love me any less. If anything it caused them to accept me more.

There is a great scene in the 2004 movie *Spanglish* where Flor, the Mexican immigrant mother, and her twelve-year-old daughter, Cristina, have an argument. The daughter has picked up some less-than-lovely American attitudes, including the phrase "Leave me alone, I need space!" Flor's response is both physical and verbal. She takes Cristina by the arms, pulls her close, looks her straight in the eyes, and in a very strong voice says, "There is no space between us!" The same is true of Christ and me. There is no space between us. Sometimes I stomp off, in a childish fit of impatience and self-pity, but still he is there. I cannot escape him, because no matter where I turn, I see the trees, the sky, the birds, my children's faces. The sun still comes up and the rain still falls. I can climb into bed angry, worn out, confused, and wearily offer whispered prayers as I drift off to sleep.

And then the morning comes and I stumble to the kitchen, make my coffee, and wait. And there he is, Christ and all his mercies—they are new, ready to be again. "You are still here," I say. "Of course you are. You are the king. I am not, but I am not worthy of your love, of fresh starts. Don't you see this crack?" And his response to me is always the same, time and time again. "That crack," he says, "is not what separates us; it is what binds us. That crack is the brokenness that I am here to heal. I was cracked, broken, and battered, and resurrected, and through that Resurrection I bring you new life. Those cracks that run down your center, those cracks you want to point at to push me away, those are the cracks of grace, of new life."

I think of Elvis, a regular human whom people crowned a king, who tried to live up to the title, who futilely tried to hide all the cracks behind the house and the trophies and the hair. What if he had been at peace with all his cracks? What if we had not demanded that he appear perfect, spotless, and infallible? Would things have turned out differently for him? Christ the King came for Elvis and he came for me, and he wants us as we are, cracks and all.

And I think of Advent being right around the corner, just as it was in my junior year of college when we took that trip. The church year is about to start again, fresh and eager with the birth of the baby Jesus. We will be pulled again into the story, the story of a life so new, so humble, so vulnerable, yet so majestic, so full of glory. But here today, a week before we step into that season of waiting and birth, before we begin to travel the road once more to death and life, Crucifixion and Resurrection, we arrive at the end. We arrive to find our King. What it all leads back to—all the feasts and all the lessons, all the parties and prayers, all the saints and symbols—in the end it all leads back to Christ our King. He is the beginning and the ending and everything in between.

Maw's Fortifying Whole-Grain Almond Waffles

This is my grandmother's recipe exactly as she gave it to me. To this day she will still make these for me any time I stay with her, and she cooks them in the same waffle iron she received as a wedding gift over sixty years ago.

Ingredients

½ cup of all-purpose flour
½ cup of wheat flour
⅓ cup of unprocessed bran
2 teaspoons of baking powder
½ teaspoon of salt
1 cup of milk
1 egg
2 tablespoons of sunflower or canola oil
   Slivered almonds

Directions

Mix all ingredients until they become a smooth batter, and pour the appropriate amount into your preheated waffle maker. Bake for about 3 minutes. Check occasionally. You can replace the almonds with walnuts, pecans, blueberries, or chocolate chips.

Serve with melted butter and warm maple syrup. Makes approximately 6 4 x 4-inch waffles.

Paper Crowns

What kids (and secretly most adults) can resist donning a crown from time to time? Waffles are one of those meals that has to be made to order, which can leave everyone else at the table a little impatient. Here is a simple and easy crown craft to occupy fidgety kids and grown-ups alike while they are waiting on their breakfast.

Materials Needed

- Scrapbook cardstock cut into 12 x 3-inch strips (1 strip per crown)
- 1½ yards of ⅛-inch satin or grosgrain ribbon per crown
- Single-hole punch
- Star punch
- Scrapbook paper scraps
- Glue sticks
- Scissors

Directions

Precut your crown strips and ribbon.

If your children are old enough, have them punch out a variety of stars using the scrapbook paper scraps; if not, prepunch them. You will need about 7 stars per crown.

Also, using your single-hole punch and remaining paper scraps, make several tiny circles (think confetti).

Instruct children to glue stars and tiny circles to their crown strips using the glue stick. (I lined my stars along the top edge of the crown and then added the tiny circle dots to the middle of each star.)

When kids are finished and stars and dots are dry, glue the ends of your strip together, creating a small crown.

Punch holes on either side of the crown and run your long ribbon through the holes.

Place the crown on your child's head and tie it under the chin, tucking the ribbon behind ears to hold securely.

chapter 23

Patterns and Printables

The patterns and printables mentioned here may be found online at
www.paracletepress.com/a-homemade-year.html

List of Activities and Recipes

Acknowledgments

There are too many people to thank by name, so I hope most of you will understand being assigned to a group. To my colleagues and friends at eStem PCS, thank you for being such a wonderful encouragement. Thanks so much to the Dinner for Eight group, the Zens, the Zitas, the Playgroup, and to Lilly and Brady Hutson. You each hold part of my heart, and I would not be who I am if it were not for you. Thank you for tirelessly posing for pictures and being my guinea pigs over and over, for always being game for my increasingly crazy ideas, and for cheering me on each step of the way.

Thank you to my family at R Street Community Church, especially Mark, Kim, Brian, and Mallory. Your support, understanding, and prayers, even when I had to step away for a few months in order to get my bearings, was the greatest gift you could ever give me, and you are living proof that there is hope for the church family. Thank you to Randall Wight, my mentor and friend. Our conversations remain some of my very favorites, and I promise to come to visit more often.

Huge thanks and hugs to Tracy and Carrie for still being my friends, despite all the miles between us. Thank you for remembering our childhoods with me. Thank you to Kim Roth for reminding me that I am enough, with or without a book; thank you for always being game for sushi and a pep talk when I need it most. Thank you to Amy, who always believed this was possible and who traveled many of the journeys recorded in this book with me, hand in hand. Thank you that after all these years, my tears still matter.

Thank you to Jeanetta Darley, who added her beautiful drawings for this book's twelve days of Christmas project: you are my craft partner in crime forever and ever. Your make-do and mend attitude always makes me smile. I promise to save you a rocking chair on the porch.

Thank you also to my team of readers-in-waiting, Christine Archer and Amy Brawner-Bishop, who provided amazing feedback and hours of help. This book would not be possible without your support, help, honesty, and encouragement.

Thank you as well to Jon Sweeney, Maura Shaw, Bob Edmonson, and everyone at Paraclete Press who took a chance on me and this book and helped guide me through the process. Thank you to Phyllis Tickle for encouraging me to give it a try in the first place.

A special thank you to my sister Judea, who lived, breathed, and recorded this project with me. You are an amazing artist and friend, and this would never have happened without you by my side. You bring to life what I see in my imagination.

And finally, thank you to my family—Nathan, my boys, my parents, grandparents, and siblings: you are my roots and my branches no matter the season. Thank you for suffering and celebrating this project with me day after day, and thank you most of all of all for loving me like you do.

A HOMEMADE YEAR

About Paraclete Press

Who We Are

Paraclete Press is a publisher of books, recordings, and DVDs on Christian spirituality. Our publishing represents a full expression of Christian belief and practice—from Catholic to Evangelical, from Protestant to Orthodox.

We are the publishing arm of the Community of Jesus, an ecumenical monastic community in the Benedictine tradition. As such, we are uniquely positioned in the marketplace without connection to a large corporation and with informal relationships to many branches and denominations of faith.

What We Are Doing
Books

Paraclete publishes books that show the richness and depth of what it means to be Christian. Although Benedictine spirituality is at the heart of all that we do, we publish books that reflect the Christian experience across many cultures, time periods, and houses of worship. We publish books that nourish the vibrant life of the church and its people—books about spiritual practice, formation, history, ideas, and customs.

We have several different series, including the best-selling Paraclete Essentials and Paraclete Giants series of classic texts in contemporary English; A Voice from the Monastery—men and women monastics writing about living a spiritual life today; award-winning poetry; best-selling gift books for children on the occasions of baptism and first communion; and the Active Prayer Series that brings creativity and liveliness to any life of prayer.

Recordings

From Gregorian chant to contemporary American choral works, our music recordings celebrate sacred choral music through the centuries. Paraclete distributes the recordings of the internationally acclaimed choir Gloriæ Dei Cantores, praised for their "rapt and fathomless spiritual intensity" by *American Record Guide,* and the Gloriæ Dei Cantores Schola, which specializes in the study and performance of Gregorian chant. Paraclete is also the exclusive North American distributor of the recordings of the Monastic Choir of St. Peter's Abbey in Solesmes, France, long considered to be a leading authority on Gregorian chant.

Videos

Our videos offer spiritual help, healing, and biblical guidance for life issues: grief and loss, marriage, forgiveness, anger management, facing death, and spiritual formation.

Learn more about us at our website:
www.paracletepress.com, or call us toll-free at 1-800-451-5006.

SCAN
TO
READ
MORE

You may also be interested in the Active Prayer series...

Praying in Color: Drawing a New Path to God

Sybil MacBeth

ISBN: 978-1-55725-512-9

$16.95, Paperback

If you are word-weary, stillness-challenged, easily distracted, or just in need of a new way to pray, try "praying in color."

Making Crosses: A Creative Connection to God

Ellen Morris Prewitt

ISBN: 978-1-55725-628-7

$16.99 Paperback

The practice of making a cross takes you beyond analytic thinking and offers a way of prayer where understanding comes from doing.

Knit One Purl a Prayer: A Spirituality of Knitting

Peggy Rosenthal

ISBN: 978-1-55725-806-9

$16.99 paperback

Knitting can help you craft a deeper connection to God—as well as reduce stress, overcome losses, and form lasting friendships.

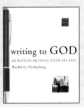

Writing to God: 40 Days of Praying with My Pen

Rachel G. Hackenberg

ISBN: 978-1-55725-879-3

$15.99 Paperback

A simple—and active—way to connect with God.
A new way to pray.